MAGIC

This work uncovers the mysteries of Magic, Natural, Mental, Ceremonial and Divine Magic, interpreting every aspect of the subject of both White and Black Magic and shows how to protect oneself against all evil forces

By

DR. A. S. RALEIGH

Late Official Scribe of the Hermetic Brotherho

A course of Private Lessons given to his personal pupils.

THE HERMETIC PUBLISHING COMPANY

3006 Lake Park Ave.   Chicago, Ill.,

CONTENTS

LESSON I

NATURAL MAGIC

Of all the different branches of Magic, Natural Magic has been most acceptable to the modern spirit. There are quite a number of scientists who are even willing to tolerate with a certain degree of respect, the study of Natural Magic, the magical aspect of the powers of nature, whereas they have nothing but the most utter contempt for any of the other branches of the subject.

Natural Magic deals with the hidden potencies of nature, of the natural powers, and is very closely connected with Astrology and Alchemy; in fact, an understanding of Magic without a study of astrology is practically impossible.

The principle on which Natural Magic rests is the Law of Hermes Trismegistus—that that which is below is equal to that which is above; that which is above is the same as that which is below. In other words, it is the law of Correspondences, the law of the Microcosm and the Macrocosm. The universe is the Macrocosm; every individual part of it, every organism, every body, whatever it may be, is the Microcosm of that Macrocosm, is the little world and corresponds in every detail to the universe only being on an infinitesimally smaller scale. This Law of Correspondences gives us an understanding of the Magical powers of Nature, because everything in the universe is in everything else. In a word, all the planets and all the signs of the Zodiac, the sun and moon, all the stars of the heavens are in each and every grain of sand,

every pebble, every flower, and because they are all in
that, because there is a small particle of each of those
bodies, that is of the same principle which is manifested
in each object, they are, therefore, able to exercise control of it, and this object, therefore, brings us into communication with the great universal force which is manifesting in and through all things.

Natural Magic as a practical art, consists in the attraction of the powers of nature so that we are able to control them, to direct them at will. It is largely the harness-
ing of the Astrological and Planetary forces. We must,
consequently, learn the Occult potencies of things. Bear
in mind, the occult potency of any object depends upon
this natural principle which is placed within it.

It should be borne in mind that not only is the object
the Microcosm of the Macrocosm of the universe, therefore, containing within it everything in all the universe,
but it is also the embodiment of certain principles. Each
plant, for instance, had embodied a certain attribute of
nature, a certain power, just as the different stars and
satellites, etc., represent certain principles. No matter
how great or how small any object may be, it has its key
note which governs all its activities; which is its genius,
and thus in a high degree, impersonates or rather indi-
vidualizes certain attributes of nature.

Natural Magic deals with the means of bringing about
the desired result, of drawing those forces, those hidden
potencies of nature. One department of it is Magical
Medicine, where drugs are administered, not because of
their physical effect, in the common sense of the term,
that is, as understood by ordinary practitioners of physic,
but rather in occult potency, in their ability to draw to
the body of the patient those forces, to make of the pa-

tient a magnet to draw the corresponding influence from the Kosmos.

Incense is burned as a part of Natural Magic because the spices that are used in making incense have certain occult potencies; they embody certain occult principles and, by burning them it will draw those principles from the world without; will concentrate them there and will also awaken the corresponding principle in the persons who smell the incense, who are in the room, and there are quite a number of fumigations which have those influences.

Natural Magic however, not only deals with those things, but it deals with the influence of music, of sound and, in fact, everything which will draw those forces and bring them to bear upon a given issue.

Not only is the Law of Correspondences true, and fundamental in Natural Magic, but also the Law of Opposites must be taken into consideration and without the Law of Opposites it would be impossible to accomplish results. The entire system of Paracelsus is really an elaboration of these two laws, the Law of Correspondences and the Law of Opposites.

What is the Law of Opposites? It is the recognition of two principles which are the two poles, as it were of nature. They are mutually attractive in the sense of being affinities, while the same principle in two objects makes them repellent. These forces, these two principles are the basis of centrifugal and centripetal force. Gravitation is nothing but the operation of centripetal force. It is due to the fact that the two objects are mutually positive and negative to each other, and because of this positive and this negative character, they attract, they gravitate toward each other. Gravitation is not due to the mere fact of objects being of the same size or anything of that kind, but it is due to the fact that one object is positive and the other negative and thus they have the tendency to rush together.

The two principles called by the Alchemists Sol and Luna or the King and the Queen, the Man and the Women—sometimes described as Gold and Silver are what we know as Electricity and Magnetism. The electro-magnetic differentiation was known to the old Magi and was employed by them; was thoroughly natural and in the works of Paracelsus it is brought out with considerable detail; and the Law of Opposites is simply these two opposing principles. Now, the Law of Correspondences means that these two principles are in everything; everything is the manifestation of these principles. Natural Magic consists in the controlling of these two principles. As an illustration of what may be accomplished by this art, think for a moment of gravitation. It is the effect of the positive and negative character of objects, that is to say it is because of their electro-magnetic character, because the one is electrical and the other magnetic. To constitute both objects electrical or both magnetic would make them cease to be positive and negative. They would become both positive, and consequently would be repellent. The Law of Gravitation can, therefore, be set at defiance by one who is able to change the polarity of the elements. One who is able to, for the time being, cause the magnetic to become electric or the electric to become magnetic is able, by reason of this fact, to entirely overcome the Law of Gravitation, to establish repulsion instead of attraction. You can, therefore, cause things to repel or to run together, as the case may be and, in fact, the wonders of the Natural Magic of the past were nothing more than the effects produced by the control of the electro-magnetic principle. It was the solving of the Law of Opposites. Nature can be absolutely controlled by the one who has the Law of Opposites under his control.

Natural Magic consists of the natural means of bringing about this result. In fact, all Magic is the effect of such control, no matter what branch it may be. Natural Magic is the use of natural forces to accomplish this control.

The use of amulets and charms, when they are used because of their natural potency is an illustration of Natural Magic. Certain metals or gems which will draw those natural forces may be employed. Colors, because of their affinity to certain natural forces, are also a part of Natural Magic; also sound, music, and everything of that kind—because music is vibration and so is everything else. The use of Mantras is also Natural Magic, although this comes more under the head of Ceremonial Magic; nevertheless they are used for the generation of certain vibrations in the ether which will, in their turn, control those forces. All Ceremonial Magic is in reality a means of bringing about Natural Magical Results, excepting when intended for the purpose of invoking or evoking the Devas.

Natural Magic consists of the impartation of certain rates of vibration to the energies of nature, generally speaking to the ether, so that the forces of electricity and magnetism are brought under control.

In order to accomplish magical feats it is first necessary to be in possession of a powerful will, one which is almost omnipotent in its positivity because by reason of the will we are able to maintain the state of outward expression, to cause the vibration of our aura to flow outward until it influences the surrounding ether.

Second, a vivid imagination by which we may form the proper mental pictures.

Third, intense concentration, stick-to-itiveness; and

Fourth, unlimited faith and confidence.

These are the four things necessary for every phase of magic. Natural Magic, however, is not so much the activity of the human will in the sense of directly influencing the electro-magnetic forces, as it is the employment of physical agents for bringing about such things, but in a broader sense Natural Magic includes every application and exercise of the forces of Nature, so that in this way it is really creative by the forming of pictures in the mind and projecting them outward, so that the vibration is transmitted to the ether. We are thus able to release them; we are thus able to control the electro-magnetic forces of nature and thus to perform the works which we have in mind.

Even the material of which one's clothing is formed has its magical effect upon nature. Certain plants and wood have the same influence. The use of Witch Hazel for locating water is not a superstition at all; it is absolutely true that certain persons are able to locate water by the use of a sprig of Witch Hazel; and why? Simply because there is an affinity between water and the Witch Hazel and it seeks its affinity. The electro-magnetic relation is very firmly established between the two. The use of Witch Hazel as a means of discovering things, deposits of ore, etc., is also on the same principle. The Divining Rod and the Magic Wand should be made of this material. There are other kinds of wood also that have their magical affinities, metals, gems, and everything of the kind.

The works of Von Helmont in the study of the magnet —the achievements which he made with magnets—being as they are, elaborations of the Paracelsean doctrine prove conclusively the two-fold character of this force which we term electro-magnetism. They prove that they are two different forces, and the wonderful results that we accomplish with the magnet justify the position taken by those people.

Later, the work of Mesmer in the development of mesmerism carries out the Natural Magical principle to a greater extent, for the foundation of mesmerism is in magnetism. It is not suggestion in the sense that that weak feature known as modern hypnotism has worked, but rather that higher and greater principle of Magnetism. Mesmer and his first disciples employed the magnetic force and through this stimulated certain faculties, produced certain conditions, and hypnotism has never been able to come anywhere near duplicating the results of Mesmer and the early Mesmerists by the use of mesmerism, and the reason it has not has been because hypnotists have not intelligently employed this great magnetic force.

Mesmerism, through Magnetism, is the control of the Law of Opposites and its application to the human organism, to the production of certain changes, the bringing to bear of certain influences upon the human body, mind and soul. It is, therefore, Natural Magic, pure and simple, and all the achievements of the mesmerists demonstrate the truth of the fundamental principles of Natural Magic. It demonstrates that mankind, the individual, embodies the Kosmic Forces of nature; that man is the Microcosm of the Universe; that every force in the universe is in man, and, by bringing those forces to bear upon the corresponding principle in man, that may be highly stimulated and man may be brought into harmony with these great natural forces; may be brought under their

control and thus, by the stimulation of those forces, the
wonderful results which we see manifested in the human
being under mesmeric control are brought about. The
same results may be achieved in any other way by the
bringing about of a state of polarity between man and
nature in precisely the same way. A mesmeric subject is
not so much a man under the control of his higher self,
as so many of the mesmerists would have us believe, but
it is rather certain faculties of man's being under abnormal stimulus from other corresponding powers in nature.
The same effect can, in a measure, be produced by a
charge of electricity, only it is very dangerous to employ
it. We should bear in mind, likewise, that there are certain drugs that will produce mesmeric effects, such
particularly as chloral, hashish, opium and drugs of
that description. The influence that is brought to bear
when a person is under their dominance is not imagin-
ative; it is absolutely real. Delirium tremens is an instance of Natural Magic from the action of intoxicating
liquors.

We see, therefore, that natural forces may be concentrated by certain agents, and, being concentrated, will
stimulate the faculties of man or animal so as to produce
certain effects.

As a matter of fact, the use of chemicals in agricul-
tural fertilizers is nothing in the world but the application of magical powers to stimulate corresponding
principles in the plant and cause growth. A current of
electricity will induce growth in the same way, by the
stimulation of the principles in the plant. All the way
through it is nothing but the operation of magical power,
that is, the application of the powers of nature unto the
production of definite results. The Law of Correspondences and the Law of Opposites, being the two-fold

operation of electro-magnetic force are the cause of Natural Magic. One able to control this operation is able to produce any kind of magical results. The various systems or divisions of Magic are simply so many methods for bringing about this result.

Natural Magic is the use of material objects, material substances, forces, etc., as a means of bringing into realization this control of those forces of nature. Anyone able to do this is a Natural Magician. All the studies of the Magi were to secure a knowledge of these laws; to understand the affinities and antipathies of the various forces in nature, the various objects, so by the use of them they would be able to secure this control of the electro-magnetic force and, through them, of the law of Sympathy and Antipathy.

LESSON II

WHITE MAGIC

The principles of Natural Magic must always be borne in mind as laying the foundation for the other phases of magic. If it were not for those principles there would be no basis for the other activities. It is because of the change of the polarity of the elements and those influences, that the other methods are able to accomplish the result. In other words, the various methods of Magic are simply the means of accomplishing the Natural Magic. They are so many instruments in the hands of Magicians to bring about the change of polarity in the elements which leads to the desired physical results.

White Magic deals with the elementals. There is both White Magic and Goeti. Goeti deals with the same forces and the same entities; but White Magic is when the purpose is not intended as being evil. While we use those powers for a good purpose the motive is good, or not, at least, evil, while in Goeti it is positively evil. The White Magic will deal with those beings when they are invoked or evoked for the purpose of accomplishing works which are relatively good.

Now, it is necessary that we should understand first the nature of the elementals which are invoked. Those elementals are generally denied in modern times, while a few centuries ago in Europe they knew they existed, and so among the Hindus to-day and in Northern Europe the belief in the elementals is universally accepted, and in the public schools they teach it. Therefore, there is more truth than poetry in those statements. There are four elements: earth, air, fire and water; as the two-fold manifestations of electricity and magnetism are each occupied by a class of elementals, nature spirits, so to speak; although in one sense they are not spirits at all; these entities occupy those elements and live in them: Gnomes, representing the principles of carbon, living in the earth; Sylphs, representing the principles of nitrogen, living in the air and wherever nitrogen is present; Undines, representing the element of hydrogen, living in the water and the hydrogenic element; the Salamander, representing the principle of fire, and as such living wherever that is present.

Remember that those elements in their highest aspect are forms of ether. Those elementals do not have any gross bodies, but they live in the forms of ether; they do not rise above it, they do not have souls or spirits, in the sense that even animals have. The animals on the physical plane have more soul than those beings; and there is little intelligence, generally speaking. They live in the element to which they belong; fairies is a term applied to all of them, indiscriminately.

Fay was applied by the Scandinavians; fay is the highest order of nature spirit, being a ruler. Fairy lore is not reliable, mostly romantic, dealing with kings and queens, etc., making it a very complicated system; there is really nothing so complicated as this. In fact, insofar as those principles are concerned, which are so emphasized by those who write on the subject, it is nonsense. The Fairies are the nature spirits, or entities of etheric elements, whose duty it is to look after and conduct the various elements and the principle to which they belong.

Now, there are beings on all the planes of nature; of course, it does not at first look natural to us to conceive of there being entities of a semi-human character who have not physical bodies to exist in. The spiritualistic view is that they are perfected human beings; some conceive them as spirits whose destiny it is to ultimately become men; and this is the idea that Benjamin Fay Mills has when he speaks of everything becoming a man— the world and everything is forever struggling up that it might become man. It is very flattering to human vanity; but the facts are that equality in the sense in which it is implied by these arguments has no place in the whole economy of the Universe. God never intended anything of that kind. It is not the destiny of worms and bugs to become men any more than it is for rocks or stones to become Saviours.

Now, everywhere in the world we find the need for the different animal organisms. We find that the coral worm or insect, which is apparently of the least consequence, has the greatest influence on the transformation of the surface of the earth.

All worms exercise the greatest influence on the earth itself. Take, for instance, the earthworms that appear to amount to nothing, they are of such a low order; if it were not for the earthworm burrowing in the earth, and thus opening up and mellowing the soil, the ground would in time get so hard and compact that cultivation would in many localities be utterly impossible. It is due to the action of worms that animal or vegetable mould is formed; and we can see if we look at it properly that things do not exist for themselves, but each being in the world is existing for the purpose of exercising a certain influence on the whole—everything is working for the universal whole.

Now, if we realize this, we then can see that it is not necessary that there should be everything progressing to something else. We absolutely deny that they have ever been anything or ever will be anything else than what they are.

Now, really what is the function of the elementals? If we can understand them, we will be able to understand something of this work, and also the manner of controlling them; that is, the ethers which later on express themselves in the gases which are their activities, and as the gases are but expressions on the lower plane of vibration of those ethers it follows consequently that to control the ether you can control the gaseous form. If you can control the earth, air, fire and water of the alchemists you can control the physical element that you see about you. Here is this great force that is vibrating all the time, there are the vibratory forces going on in nature all the time. Now, it is not true that God does everything himself. The forces were set in motion. That is, little beings were produced—these nature spirits, these elementals—for the purpose of working in that element to keep it going properly. Now, they are in operation conducting those elements.

The Salamanders have a being of the nature of fire; that is metaphysical fire, and by their activities they control that principle; and the Sylphs and Undines have the same relation to air and water and the Gnomes to carbon or earth, and they also govern the development of the various minerals in the earth.

The statement of the old Mythologists of "Vulcan's Workshop" has direct reference to the activities of the Gnomes. The work is being done there now, and the superstitions about the dwarfs working under ground forging things are not fiction but are really true. The activities of these elementals are employed in the development of these different minerals, which are produced out of carbon by reason of the activities of these beings.

It has been known to occult chemists and astrologers that gold, for instance, is the product of the masculine positive activity of the Solar force, while Silver is produced in the same way by the Feminine, negative activé of the Moon. But the activities of those principles are governed by the Gnomes.

Now, these elementals are absolutely unmoral. There has never been discovered any trace of a moral character; they are workers, their place in the world's economy is that of merely mechanical beings; they are totally devoid of character. They may become very much attached to a person, to a being with a soul, they may serve a person very faithfully and do anything that person may want them to do, and they will do it without any thought of its being right or wrong. They may become friendly; in other words, they simply have the feeling of friendship. Their character is very well illustrated by that of the Italian Bandits—they will become friendly with a person, and, if an injury is done to him, they will cut the throat of the one doing the injury without any question of the merits of the case; he has injured their friend, and this is enough. Their only feeling is one of friendship for a person, they have no higher feeling. The same is true in the way of the elementals, but a good deal more so, because the Italian bandit had at one time a conscience which perhaps a life of lawlessness blunted or destroyed, but the elemental never had anything of the kind, but has always been by nature entirely unmoral. Therefore, they can be used to do evil just as easily as good, but to do good will not place the Magus anything like so much under their control as to do evil will, and the attachment will not have to be so strong to induce them to serve in a work which is not for a purely selfish purpose.

You may wonder why they become so much attached to people. Because they themselves are soulless, and they know that mankind has a spiritual principle which they lack; so by attaching themselves to a man in order to vampirize him of this they thus raise themselves above the ordinary level. A great deal of the witch-craft proceedings were due to the attachment these little beings had for human beings, particularly women. You will find quite a good deal along this line in different works, especially in Michilett's work, La Sarcierie, who treats it in a good deal of the spirit of the French skeptic; nevertheless it is quite interesting. They are known to become quite attached to women who are down in the mouth, who are discouraged, and often go away and come back and find their housework done.

In Denmark there are people who claim they have seen the dwarfs who live under the ground and sometimes their shovels or picks get broken and need mending, and they leave them out on the hillside somewhere, and when they go back the next morning perhaps, they find them repaired. And there is something peculiar about it. Those people who have the reputation of dealing with these elementals have a great deal better crops than those who don't. In parts of Scandinavia there are places where these good, pious Lutherans will leave out certain dishes for the elves to eat, and it is gone the next morning, too. Now, in Scotland lots of the Highlanders to this day leave a croft, a small piece of land, which is never tilled, for "the good people." Probably 20,000 acres of land, all told, is left to the "good man," in a country where there is not half enough land to furnish the crops and the people are three times as poverty-stricken as they are in England. As it is, Scotland is a wild, mountainous country for the most part, good for nothing but raising cattle. In spite of all that, there are some thousands of acres of ground that are left to the ''good people.''

Now we contend that wherever there is an universally accepted doctrine, anything that is accepted to the extent of the sacrificing of their pecuniary interests, there is a measure of truth in it. We do not believe that the Scots, those common-sense, practical people, the hardest bargain-drivers in the world, etc., would cling to a belief for ages unless there is a great fact back of it, and also one which is being continually verified—people of that type would not hold on in spite of changing their religion, if there were no truth in it, unless it had been demonstrated that the Fairies were good neighbors, and that it would be best to be on good terms with them. When the Highlanders threw over the Catholic religion, they simply converted the Fairies right along with them into the Protestant church.

In the country of Scotland, (in the cities it is not true at the present time) in Ireland, in Wales, in Denmark, Sweden, Norway, Russia, Poland, part of France, and, we are told, part of Germany, (we cannot say positively as to Germany) the belief in the Fairies is still as strong as it ever was; and there is bound to be truth underlying it, or it would not have the strength and tenacity that it has in those countries. And note here that those people who hold to those beliefs of folk-lore, and the like, are more psychical than the other nations; they are the people who have attained a certain psychical development in spite of the trend of modern civilization.

Now the fact that the belief in the Fairies is found to coincide with the possession of psychical faculties adds a strong presumption of the truth of their claims, notwithstanding how impossible the belief may appear to the people who have no such development. In other words, the statement most of these people make, particularly in Ireland, that they have seen the fairies, is true. They have a very strong conviction of the matter; it is not guesswork. This conviction they could not possibly develop except by personal experience.

The Fairies, by reason of their willingness, even their anxiety to work for people, in fact to have a human master, make it very easy for a person to acquire magical power if he goes about it in a certain way. There are certain rules to be followed.

Why are the Fairies so anxious to serve men and women? Because by establishing a tie between themselves and the human being they can draw to themselves the magnetism of that man or woman, who is their master or mistress, and, therefore, raise themselves to a higher plane than they otherwise would attain. In this way they can develop some of those powers which are rudimentary in themselves, but are strong in man. If they are able to do this it is not very good for the man or woman who is working in connection with them. You have, of course, read of stories about persons being destroyed by the Fairies, and these people, who have dabbled in magic to a certain extent have been destroyed by the Fairies when their powers have been sapped; and remember if a person is thus consumed by the Fairies he does not simply leave his body and go to the astral plane, because it is his higher principles that are being sapped, not his physical. They don't want his physical or his etheric double. They already have astral vehicles; it is his mind and his soul and spirit that are being sapped. So there is always danger of something of that kind

happening, and that is really the underlying principle
of why the church opposed any intercourse with Fairies;
they think they are devils, etc., yet they intuitively
recognize the danger of dealing with them.

Now, there are even cases of where a sex union between those beings and humans has taken place. There
are cases which have been reported, and which are un-
mistakably true, of sailors for instance, and other beings
who have fallen in love with the Undines.

It is all those matters of magical power which are
brought about by union, or anything of that kind, which
are always detrimental to the persons who are practicing
it, and always beneficial to the Spirits with whom they
deal. That is the reason why they are so accommodating,
doing something for the humans.

In works of Italians, dealing with Fairy Lore, they
speak of the Fairies proposing to help people if they
would give them their souls. Now, of course, the priests
claim they are devils and want them to give them their
souls and want them to go to Hell. It was not for that
purpose at all. It is simply giving up their soul-energies
to the Elementals and allowing them to live in that soul
force until it is consumed. But they are willing to cooperate and to help a person along in many respects just
so they get that advantage: if they cannot get you to
turn over your soul to them. Your society is very advantageous to them. Whenever you take the Fairies
into your service they must be kept at work. When the
Fairies no longer are employed they turn against the
person who had them under his control.

Now, with those entities, if they can be made to do
what you tell them to do you can work wonders. For
instance, if you have Undines you can make it rain any
time you want to, just so you give them time to gather

moisture and condense it. On the other hand, if you have Gnomes under your control, they will show you where deposits of ore are to be found, and thus you may get rich in mining, and the like. If you have the Salamanders, you may control the lightning and thunder, etc. The Sylphs will give you control of the wind and the storm. It was by control of these elementals that Christ was able to stop the storm, as it says: "He rebuked the winds," which would be senseless if addressed to the winds themselves, but quite plain if addressed to intelligent entities who control those natural activities. It was not that he was a Magus and had the elementals attached to him, but they all recognized their master, as everything else did about that time, except the Pharisees.

By having those entities under your control you can produce anything which you desire; they will bring about the changes in the atmosphere wherever it may be. There are some persons who are found to be successful mariners on the sea; when they go out in a ship, that ship will never sink if they are on it. The Fairies recognize something in him which establishes the state of rapport with themselves, there is a strong affinity between him and the Undines, who feel that, and thus assist him, and they recognize their natural master and obey. Miners and prospectors who are lucky are those persons who have the carbon element in them so strong that the Gnomes naturally feel their affinity and cooperate with them and work with them; and those persons, on the other hand, who are fortunate in everything connected with the air and the winds have their affinity with the Sylphs. The persons who are manufacturing, smelting, are in harmony with the Salamanders; those are of the nature affinities.

Charms and talismans are due to the influence they have upon certain elementals, for certain reasons they give power over the element they are workers in; the charm gives you power to control those elementals.

There are two methods of performing magic. These are invocation and evocation.

Invocation is the method used when you ask, and evocation when you command. Evocation is never safe; but invocation should never be practiced, because you are placing yourself in a meek attitude, you are placing yourself under an obligation. You are a being having a spiritual and soul nature and being capable of rising to the highest contemplation of the Divine, praying to a being who is totally devoid of intelligence; they are handy craftsmen, machinicians, but nothing higher.

LESSON III

GOETIA

Goetia is practically the same as White Magic, with the exception that in White Magic, the person is acting from the standpoint of a relatively good intention, that is, his intention is not malevolent; but he goes to work and produces phenomena and accomplishes the work that he has in mind while his motive is good—it is to positively benefit some one, or to carry out a work in which he is interested, which he believes in; he may use the power in the interest of what is a good cause. The point of difference is this—the devotee of White Magic is acting from conscientious principles while the practitioner of Goetia knows he is committing a crime. He does the work that he does knowing that it is not right to do it, and he is actuated by selfish motives.

Now, the devotee of White Magic may destroy life at times, (not likely, but the time comes when it may be done). He is doing it for the human race, he is doing it for the good of the people who are oppressed. The devotee of Goetia has no thought of what is right or anything of that kind. He has a certain purpose that he wishes to realize, knowing the criminal character of the work, but going ahead and doing it. Unless the element of pure selfishness is involved in some form, it is not Goetia. Goetia may be practiced for revenge. The person may be made, by the use of magical power, to do things for the purpose of revenge. He may want to administer to his animal passions; he may want to gratify his sensuality; and when he has gratified his sensuality then he is ready to let things go. But he uses this for the purpose of gratifying his sensuality, and we know of a case of that kind here in the City of Chicago, of a prominent man who uses magic for the purpose of seducing other men's wives. Now, when magical power is employed for any sensual purpose, when the elementals are employed for the purpose of administering to those passions, or for revenge, or when a person will employ magical power for higher purposes, that is, to secure supernormal powers, or when a person pays him for the use of his magical power, it is always Goetia. There are professional magicians who make use of those powers merely as a business.

At one time the standard of legal ethics was very high; and the lawyer was considered part of the court, he was really an officer of the court and was working in the interests of justice. It was his duty to see that justice was guaranteed. But the spirit of modern law practice is that he represents his client's interests; whatever his client's interests are they are his interests. Now, the Goetic Magicia acts in the very same spirit. "I represent my employer," he says. "If my employer wants me to do a little magic, to invoke the elementals in his service, and pays me my price, it is nothing to me." That is the spirit; it is followed as a business. Now, there are practitioners of Goetia who, without any grievance against you, will go to work and destroy you simply because they are being paid to do it. It is merely a matter of business with them. They belong to the class of thugs, cut-throats and assassins. Now, all these characteristics represent the character of the black magician. The white magician never receives pay for performing magical work. This does not mean a person who is doing something connected with occultism, but a High Magus who deals with the elementals will not receive pay for it. You may give him anything you want as a gift, but he will not receive money for that which he does. Now, the reason he will not do it is quite obvious, if you will consider a moment. If he receives a price he places himself in debt to help you, under obligation to do what you want him to do. By simply invoking them, in a word, his conscience is left perfectly clear and free. Therefore, he is able to go ahead and do what he thinks is right. The practitioner of Goetia receives a definite fee for invoking the elementals and accomplishing certain work; even he is paid on condition that he is successful. Therefore, it is to his interest to demonstrate success, and consequently the temptation is so strong that he is not able to resist it. Now, in the practice of Goetia it is the outcropping of selfishness. The person is acting in the interest of himself, or to gratify his revenge, or something of that kind; he is not stimulated by benevolence. The essence of White Magic is disinterested benevolence, while the essence of Goetia is interested selfishness. Now, whatever partakes of this element belongs to the class of Magic to which the element pertains—that is the only difference between the two. In both they are using the same elementals. In fact, the same elemental may be invoked for Goetic Magic who is invoked for White Magic. One person may employ a certain element to-night for White Magic and some one else may use the very same one for Goetia. Remember the elementals have absolutely no morals; being absolutely unmoral they have no appreciation of moral relations. Consequently, they will lend themselves to one activity just as quickly as they will to another. It is solely the personality, the personal power and control of the Magus which influences them, without any thought whatever as

to his character, only in this: that the elementals, of
course, recognize when it is selfishness and when it is
disinterestedness. They will obey the strength of the
Magus no matter what it may be, whether it be disinterestedness or selfishness. However, there is a measure of
resentment that they feel against a man that will invoke
them and use their power purely to his own selfish ends.
They have a measure of reverence in spite of the fact that
they have no morality themselves. No matter how dis-
agreeable a person may be, no matter if he is immoral
himself, he respects the moral man, the man who is sincere and honest and who believes in himself. We have
heard the expression used by certain men of the worst
character in life to priests, for instance, who were sincere
and they were infidels, who had been brought up as Catholics: "I do not believe in your religion; I do not believe
in your Bible; I do not believe in your church; I do not
believe in your Christ, but by God, I believe in you."

This is the attitude—no matter how discreditable a
man may be he appreciates and recognizes sincerity.
When he knows what he is doing is wrong and is using
the elemental as a tool for advancing these selfish motives, where the elemental is unable to help himself, his
resentment is aroused. Now, when the elementals realize
that the Magus is acting selfishly, actuated by purely
selfish motives, is using them as tools and not for higher
purposes, that he is producing misery, and while the
elemental is unmoral yet he is not hateful, he does not
really like to produce misery; in fact, there are cases
where they have really been instrumental in helping people; he does not like the idea of producing misery. Now,
when he sees that he is being used for purposes of this
kind, his resentment is aroused—but not enough to re-
fuse to be instrumental in this kind, but far enough that

he will hate the person who is using him in that way. Now, in the same way, we see the elemental while he goes ahead doing the bidding of the Magus who invokes him, yet there is a measure of resentment instead of respect, there is hatred, although there is fear. Just as soon as they dare do it, they will turn against their former master; in fact, the closing of Bulwer-Lytton's Strange Story gives the account of the destruction of a master who had ruled the elementals for a period of time, but who had sunk so low that he was no longer their master, and because he dared to evoke them, they all turned upon him. The reason is that while a person is acting with disinterestedness he has the respect and esteem of the elementals, so to speak, as their love is different—the difference is as the tyrant whom the subject serves because they fear him. The White Magus, on the other hand, is the king whom the subjects serve out of patriotism. That is the difference between the two classes.

Now, in the practice of all of this kind of magic—be it white or black—the principal power or force consists in the ability to dominate and control those lesser beings; those elementals must be directed, must be dominated and controlled. To do this, it is necessary that the person's will-power should be almost infinite; his will must never waver; he must always direct, never receive from them, and while directing them, keep them busy at the same time and hence maintain his superior force. If he never gets a group of elementals whose power is great, when he ceases to become a master, the very moment their combined force is greater than his individual force, then they are able to dictate terms, to direct the course of his activities.

Now, remember, the elementals themselves cannot act among men except as they are either evoked or invoked.

The elementals can never come into touch with the human family until some human being calls them up. Now, when they get control of a man they proceed to make him call them whenever they want to be called, to force him to invoke, so he is usually being run, acting as a channel for their activity. Now, the great danger is that the Magus will sooner or later come under their control. Almost all magicians come under the control of the elementals sooner or later, and the Black Magus much sooner than the other.

Now, the Black Magus comes into that condition where he himself must make a compact with them, so to speak; he must make certain concessions to the elementals. This practice of Goetia is where he must submit to them in a way and make certain concessions. You must remember that the thing that controls them is strength and force. Now, selfishness undermines the force; the strength of character disappears. This force is no longer there, and owing to its absence he is now the tool of the elementals whom he has invoked, because he is no longer able to cause them to come under his control.

Now, what are the forces, the features, in a word, which go to make up the Magus, whether he be practicing White Magic or Goetia? Those forces are precisely the same. They are, first of all, vivid imagination. They must be able to make the mental picture, and they must have an almost omnipotent will that will cause itself to manifest in the surrounding elements. Unwavering confidence in his power to accomplish that which he wishes to accomplish without fail. Fourth, he must have the power of almost infinite concentration upon this object; and fifth, the power to continue in this state of patience and expectation. Now, those are the forces that are necessary to accomplish any kind of magical activity. Now, if the person is practicing Goetia he must have selfishness. The more selfishness he has the greater is his power. If he is not utterly selfish, if he has pity for his victim, if for one moment he hesitates, he weakens his power; consequently, in order to succeed it is absolutely necessary that all pity be trampled out, every fear and also compassion in his nature. That is the reason that this practice is destructive of virtue, the reason that men go to the dogs, so to speak—because they *must* do this, or else they will weaken their power. At the moment of invoking if he weaken so that he fail to concentrate they get hold of him. Therefore, he must not weaken, he must not show any pity for the victim. Now, this remorseless character, of course, gives him power for the time being, but it makes him more and more unmoral; it finally eliminates all moral sense in his being; he reaches the point when he is an unmoral being, as far as his life is concerned.

Now, the thing that inspires the elementals with the greatest respect is man's moral and spiritual nature. Some people have believed that the fairies are always supposed to have a high degree of antagonism for religion. That is not true; although they have no spirituality themselves, yet they recognize the superiority which man's spiritual nature gives to him; and Bulwer-Lytton's Strange Story shows that the thing that aroused their indignation was because Margrave, after his soul was lost still dared to command them. It is man's spiritual nature that makes him the master of the elementals. It is because he has a principal they have not got or at least in the degree that he has, because he is a rational and spiritual being that he is able to command them and they obey. Now, they obey him because they want to get as much as possible of that element. As he goes along in this spiritual relation, this spiritual activity, we see that in time he loses it, because of what he is doing; he is becoming unmoral, and as he becomes unmoral that distinction is removed; he is approaching nearer and nearer to the elementals, and is approaching the same plane, and he is, also, undermining his spirituality; he is approaching the time when he will have no moral spirit. Now, having lost that distinction, that which distinguishes him from them, they lose respect for him and resent the idea of being commanded by him. He now only has those powers which they have in a way, and now it is a struggle between the two for power. Sooner or later he must surrender and be the tool in the hands of the elementals, or else he will be destroyed; and this is the fate of every practitioner of Goetia—he is sooner or later to go insane, to die a violent death or else to become the slave of the elementals. The elementals who have been invoked by him become his masters instead of his slaves. They will destroy him or subject him to their authority. And, remember, that when he gets in this position, when this surrender is made, he has to surrender to a group of entities who do not have any feeling of gratitude toward him, they are without any high feeling—he simply acted from the standpoint of pure selfishness. Remember this, that the elementals never serve any being except for the sake of gain; they do not do it unless they get help themselves.

Suppose in the first place they are serving for the sake of gain, you must make it profitable for them to be faithful or they will not be. In the second place, they serve you for your strength of will. They know this, and they will consequently take the first opportunity to get the upperhand; they will take the first opportunity to use it for their own purposes. Now, they are quite ready and anxious to do their work on the physical plane among men. They can only do it through a human being, and they want to come on to the physical plane—that is something common to all astral beings or spirits—they want to act on the physical plane, and they cannot do it direct; they must do it through the instrumentality of some human being. Therefore, they proceed to bring about those conditions. They will serve the human being as long as he can give them what they wish; the very moment that it is safe they will subject him to their authority, something resembling obsession. All the stories about the dwarfs, fairies and elves are really true, in a great measure. Of course, not those stories, as we said, that delve in their religious worship. They will take control wherever they can, and they can do it sooner or later if intercourse with them is kept up long enough; particularly if Goetia is practiced.

The distinctively human characteristics which will manifest in a moral spiritual life are the ones which give man his power to control them; and as those characteristics must be sacrificed, must be eliminated, in order that man can get those powers, the very intercourse with them—especially in Goetia—is undermining the superior man. When that superiority is dropped, whenever it has disappeared, then the power to control soon leaves the person and he becomes subjected. It is for this reason that Goetia is always spoken of as "Soul Destroying." It reduces the human being to the level of the elementals, he is more or less subjective, and therefore must come under the power and domination of the entities whom he has invoked.

The man who does not want to be the slave to those entities had better have nothing to do with them; particularly he had better never invoke them through selfish motives. The power of control will leave him, and then they take the direction of affairs in their hands, and the human ruler, instead of being the ruler any longer becomes the ruled, and is directed by them. You must bear in mind that they will take advantage of every opportunity to assume definite control as they resent the idea of being controlled; they want some one to do what they want done; they simply want to run things and have it their own way, and they get tired of being restrained.

He weakens himself by the life he leads, destroys those very faculties which enabled him to master them, and he, also, destroys the respect which they formerly had for him; they get to feeling a kind of familiarity.

Is it not possible for a human being to become somewhat lower in degree than an elemental?

He may become lower in moral relations, because an elemental is not simply immoral, he is unmoral. While a human being may become antagonistic to morality itself, he may become devilish, that desire for evil perceived when he delights in those things just because they are evil. The elemental is always merely indifferent to morality, he is never against it; but a man may sink until he is antagonistic to morality.

LESSON IV

MENTAL MAGIC

By Mental Magic we mean that Magical Power which may be exercised by the use of thought forms to perform certain actions, and the ability of a person with a strong, positive mind to project those forms into the Mental Plane and force them to perform certain functions.

A thought form is something more than a thought. It is, as a matter of fact, a body of Manas, forming an organism ensouled by a thought. The ensouling thought, consequently, gives character to the form. It is much more powerful than the thought because all that vast body of Manas is moved by the thought exercising all the forces latent within it. The complete character of the thought form is due to the thought which ensouls it. That thought gives character to the form and thus causes it to act consistently with that ensouling thought.

Many religious ceremonies have been performed for the express purpose of producing thought forms and where a number of persons are concentrating their minds on one and the same thought, they build up a thought form of tremendous force, because if the thought be the same no matter how many minds project it, it will simply accumulate the strength of all those minds, still remaining one thought, gathering up the Manas which is set free by the thinking of that multitude of persons, also gathering up the Manas from the Mental Plane which its vibration enables it to gather and forming a body for itself. It thus becomes powerful.

(35)

These thought forms may, in the course of time, become visible, so that not only clairvoyants, but ordinary persons will be able to see them. The form which they assume is that of the thought, or more properly the idea which is held in the consciousness of the persons who are doing the thinking. Consequently, were we to behold a Temple service or a Church service, where a great deal of devotion, a great deal of emotional concentration and also a great deal of intellectual concentration were united in the service we would see rising a thought form which would be the type of worship of the service and teaching in that service. All the devotion of the public and also of private individuals goes to form thought forms possessing that character ensouled by that thought. Such thought forms manifest themselves and continue in operation for a very long period of time; and not only this, but they work on the mental plane, propagating the same thought that ensouled them. They are not simply passive or magnetic, but, on the contrary, are self directing. They have, therefore, individuality as it were, and are intelligent entities. This individuality is determined by the thought which ensouls them. Thought forms generated in a religious service have the same religion as the people at that service, consequently they will continue to propagate that religion. Thought forms generated in a political caucas, have the same political opinions and will act out those opinions, will propagate them and will influence other minds in that direction. Wherever they go, they will continue to maintain those principles.

Inasmuch as the Thought Form is absolutely unprogressive, never changes, but continues in the direction imparted to it by the thought ensouling it at the time such thought is first projected, it is consequently pre-eminently a fossil. We must, therefore, be very careful in the formation of thought forms because we cannot change their character after once they have been produced.

Many persons, while in the lucid state, see thought forms on the Mental Plane and assume them to be entities, spirits or something of that kind, but this is a mistake. The Thought Form is purely a mental structure built up by reason of the powerful projection of thought when at the same time the form was associated with it. For this reason it follows that Abstract Thinking will not produce Thought Forms. In order to produce a Thought Form the thought must be associated with an idea of form, and when we are thinking abstractly we do not associate form with our thought, therefore we do not produce the form.

It has been stated by a great many that we see things which do not exist; that by vividly concentrating the imagination, by willing to see a certain thing, we see it whether it exists or not, but this is an error. The form does exist and this concentration of the imagination has really produced a form that is seen in this state of concentration; we simply discover something that we have created. Many persons have such power of concentration that they are able to produce Thought Forms that are immediately visible to them—their own ideas and thoughts; they are often ensouled forms, and thus they are peopling the surrounding atmosphere with forms appearing to be real beings. The so-called hallucinations are quite often nothing more nor less than the rendering visible, forms generated by the thinking.

But the all important point is the fact that these forms work; that they produce effects, stimulating corresponding thought in other beings, causing others to think the same thought, thus carrying on the work which they have had begun in themselves. This is not simply spontaneous telepathy as is the activity of thoughts to stimulate corresponding thought in the minds of others. Thought form has a personality which is as definite in kind, though, of course, infinitely less in degree, as that of a man living upon the earth, which works in that particular line and has no other characteristic; it is an enthusiast with that particular aim, having no other object in life, having a perfect mania, in fact, for that particular tendency which is imparted to it by the ensouling thought.

It should be borne in mind, therefore, that every Thought Form means another enthusiast for that particular line of thought and will work in that direction most zealously and most tenaciously. It is for this reason that buildings, temples, etc., saloons—whatever the character of the building may be, each has its mental atmosphere, its Genius, so to speak, which is the accumulated Thought Form, and in time it becomes most powerful; it becomes a giant, dominating all the other Thought Forms and the thinking of the people who come in there. Each country has a genius, built up in this particular way and the Genii of the Orient are true; what we read about the Genii is perfectly true. They are those gigantic Thought Forms that have been built up by the concentration of mind of hundreds and thousands of people, those Thought Forms because of their affinity, merging, running together and becoming one. As they have the same thought ensouling them, they lose themselves in that one dominating thought and, therefore, all lose themselves in one Thought Form, manifesting its power in the highest conceivable degree.

When the thought is accompanied by emotion in the projection of a form, it not only becomes a Thought Form, not only has a Mental Body, but it has also an Astral Body and this is able to descend to the Astral Plane and stimulate corresponding emotions. In this way it builds up those forces more and more.

It should be borne in mind that Thought Forms which are artificial elementals really have a motive in stimulating corresponding thought and emotion, because when they have stimulated thought and emotion of their own order in the minds and hearts of those persons whom they are able to reach, they are enabled to draw this into their own being and thus replenish the Mental Body with the thought and the Astral Body with the emotion so that they prevent their death and are able to perpetuate their lives. It is, therefore, necessary for the continuity of their being that they continue to influence the thought and emotion of people. Not only is the thought and emotion of men built into these Thought Forms, but also those of animals; in fact, animals produce Thought Forms. Great musicians produce Thought Forms likewise, while they are producing music. The music is taking that form and exercising its influence. Not only, however, do the Thought Forms have Astral Bodies and Mental Bodies, but when thought is vitalized, becomes magnetic, as we sometimes express it, more properly vital, with a great deal of Prana, it has the effect of transmitting to the Thought Form life force, so that it is not only intelligent and emotional but it lives, possessing an individual life of its own. Now, if a Thought Form can get in connection with the Ether sufficiently to form itself an Etheric Double, it can descend to the physical plane and operate there and, as a matter of fact when blood is thrown out and vibrates, they are able to take ether from the blood, form Etheric Bodies and descend to the Etheric Range of the Physical Plane. It is for this reason that those Thought Forms which have been built up by the worship of certain heathen nations stimulate the idea of bloody sacrifices; having the sacrifices offered that they may use the blood to form bodies for themselves. Fresh blood is of great service to these Thought Forms, these artificial elementals, in enabling them to continue their existence on the physical plane, and so, many of the bloodiest sacrifices have been performed under the stimulus of the Thought Form.

A highly developed Thought Form can become a full fledged god and demand sacrifices, make revelations and everything of the kind because of the great mental force that is stored up there. He makes revelations in the sense that he suggests thought corresponding to the character of the thought projected into his being. It should, therefore, be observed that the revelations coming from these divinities are invariably confirmatory of the worship that has been going on for ages. They are, therefore, the production of the Thought Form that has accumulated from the thinking of the worshippers for many generations and are absolutely unmerciful to the innovator and the one who would introduce a new religion, because they know that their existence is dependent upon the continuing of that line of thought on the part of their worshippers, consequently if a new religion is introduced, a new form of worship brought about and a new line of thinking started up, the people will cease to think from that point of view and the result will be that the thoughts that will be generated will not be in harmony with the thought ensouling them, therefore they will not be able to draw them to themselves and they will perish; consequently, they fight for their lives and when the victims are destroyed they can draw their blood to themselves and maintain their physical existence. We read in many of the stories of Scotland and England, Ireland and some other countries, in the fairy lore, descriptions of cases where fairies have arisen from certain emotions, some one dropped a tear, for instance, and a fairy sprang up. There is a measure of truth in these statements. These fairies are the product of great compassion, great grief, of sympathy or a case of love when the emotion is poured forth, and poured forth when a form is held in the consciousness, while the mind is polarized upon the idea of some form. The result is, the emotion or astral substance poured forth under this feeling becomes an artificial elemental possessing that character; or perhaps it is a thought; one thinking along certain lines, reasoning out a certain problem and it takes so much Manas. He generates a fairy, an artificial elemental embodying the character of that thought. In this way these elementals are formed and for a long period of time carry on their work; work consistently with that line of thought, with the character imparted to them at the time.

Now, the reason why these fairies are described as being great and exalted characters, far superior to humanity, is that they are generated by an almost superhuman amount of emotion or thought, by a concentration of mind which is not normal; when the whole being is thrown into the thought or the feeling; man is transcending himself and thus they get this force.

Many of the forms that are resorted to in Magic are resorted to for the purpose of forming artificial elementals, Thought Forms, whether one realizes this motive or not. For instance, you will make up your mind that you want a certain calamity to happen to a man. When you have made up your mind to that end, you may, for instance, have a pile of stones and every day you pass, throw a stone on the pile, wishing that a certain calamity will happen to the man at the time that stone strikes the pile, and thus picturing the idea, thus helping to form the picture of the calamity. Or on the other hand, you may picture some good happening to a person in this way, and you simply make the motion in order to help the concentration of the mind. But any method, no matter what it may be, that helps the concentration of the mind, that helps to form the picture, will help form the artificial elemental. The worship of Mary by the Roman Catholic devotees has been instrumental in creating several million Virgin Marys, having that character and carrying on the work. The saints are really not the saints whom the Catholics worship but the ones they create by their worshipping, for saint worship is instrumental in creating a vast multitude of saints. Whenever we worship heroes or rulers, whoever it may be, we are creating them simply by the activity of that devotion, that building, and when man has formed in his consciousness an image, a high ideal, and always keeps that before him, he is producing artificial elementals, the exact duplicate of that ideal. Thus his ideal is being reproduced continually. The entire character of the Catholic Church has been largely the work of these ideals, not simply the effect that they have on the ones who are doing the thinking, but in a far greater degree in the creation of artificial elementals having that same character. The Jesuit has always formed in the mind a picture of the ideal which is Ignatius Loyola and thus millions of Ignatius Loyolas have been produced. In this way, whatever one's ideals may be, he is continually generating Thought Forms that embody that ideal. The use of images and pictures by the Catholics and some other religions has the effect of always associating the ideal with a certain form, and certain appearances. The result is, Thought Forms are produced, having that appearance, that form, that will appear and will be real.

Mental Magic is the deliberate, systematic and intentional production of Thought Forms; of thinking for the express purpose of generating artificial elementals, having the character attributed to them by the thought. The Mental Magus goes about Magic with the express purpose of producing these Thought Forms so that they may work out his will, may carry out the purpose he has in mind. He produces them for a certain purpose, the accomplishment of certain ends, and so he tells them what to do at the time he produces them, this being the only time when he has this authority over them and is able to tell them what to do.

Mental Magic is, therefore, one of the most potent branches of Magical Practice and consists of the Creation of THOUGHT FORMS, endowing them with a definite thought which is the expression of a system and will itself carry out the end which the Magus has in view. It may be good or evil. If it is sufficiently implanted in the form, if the form is ensouled with a thought sufficiently definite, it will become a consistent laborer, untiring in its efforts to promote the end in view at the time of its generation.

LESSON V

BLACK MAGIC

Black Magic is that department of Mental Magic employed solely for evil purposes. The Mental Magi may make use of Thought Forms without any desire to do evil. It may be employed for a benevolent purpose, for the accomplishment of some Kosmic end, but in Black Magic the forms are made from a purely selfish intentoin.

Like Goetia, Black Magic may be resorted to for the purpose of bettering one's condition at the expense of another, of gratifying one's lust, of securing revenge for a real or fancied injury, of obtaining power over persons or of gratifying one's hatred against the human race. In any case it is exercised for a purely selfish or evil end.

Inasmuch as the Black Magus employs Thought Forms for evil purposes, his art consists in the systematic production of those forms. The various methods employed are so many methods, used specifically for the generation of those Thought Forms.

It should be borne in mind that in order to aid in the forming or generating the Thought Form it is very often advisable to use different means of fixing the attention. The Thought Form is the result of a Mental Picture, a picture made with great vividness. It requires a powerful imagination, deep concentration, to make these forms with success, and any means assisting in the formation of the picture is of value. The picture must be one of the action which is to transpire. Merely picturing in a general way will not be sufficient. You must form a distinct picture of the definite action, a picture which will form a Thought Form of that specific character. If you can succeed in accomplishing this you will be able to realize the end.

One of the old methods in use for quite a long time was to take a picture of the person and go out to where two roads crossed, nail it up, and go every day and strike the nail one blow with a hammer, turn your back and go away without looking back. This was supposed to kill the person. There was a man in Georgia years ago, who got the idea that a certain old woman, Aunt Pennie Crue, who was called a witch, had bewitched him, so he got an artist to make a picture of her, carried it out one day and nailed it up, starting one nail in the head and the other in the chest. Every day he went and struck it a lick. The day he started the nails she took down with a pain in her head and chest, and the day the nails were driven up, she died. This is a fair illustration of the method employed. By inserting nails in that particular place you are continually projecting a Thought Form representing the affliction in that part of the body, and the result will be that influence that will cause a sickness in the head or breast or wherever it may be.

Another method is to take virgin wax and make an image of the person, and, for instance, stick pins in this image. This will help to form the picture and the result will be the person represented by this wax image will suffer exactly as though you were sticking pins in his body. You may cut gashes in it, and if your imagination be sufficiently vivid, gashes will be found in the body of your victim. You may put poison in the wax image and if the picture be sufficiently clear, the Thought Form will be produced that will act upon the patient in exactly the same way as will that poison if administered direct. The story of the attempt to kill King Duff of Scotland is an illustration of these methods. King Duff was wasting away; nobody could tell what was the matter with him. His physician could not find any cause for his illness, yet he was sweating to death—literally wasting away; got so weak he could barely stand, and it was finally decided that he was bewitched. At last they found two old women in a hut where one of them had a wax image of Duff attached to a spit, and was basting it over the fire and continually chanting while she held it there: "As this wax melts away by the heat, even so may Duff waste away." These women were put to death for practicing witchcraft on majesty.

By melting the wax, causing it to waste, you may also form the picture of the victim wasting away and that form will thus be generated which will act upon him in that way. It should be borne in mind that the only use of these images and pictures is to help fix the attention, and help the concentration of the mind so that the Thought Forms will be produced. If we are able to fix the attention with equal vividness without them, nothing of the kind is necessary, but we must have the picture in order to the generation of the Thought Form, and the image is in most cases advantageous as a means of generating the Thought Form. The chants and invocations, songs, etc., that are resorted to also, by the practitioners of Black Magic, are intended to help in forming the picture. It is not that there is any spiritual force in the formula; it is simply a means of generating the requisite Thought Form and thus when the words are employed they are intended to help fix the attention. The forms and ceremonies are required to be gone through in a certain way because they will thus gain a sanctity which they did not previously possess, and as this sanctity in maintained, one will have the imagination more highly excited while pronouncing them than he would with a formula destitute of such sanctity. It is for this reason that the Black Magus in writing a formula usually tells the devotee of the art that if he repeats it to another he will lose the power. By fearing to lose it by imparting it to anyone else, he thinks of it much more highly than he would otherwise, expects it to work wonders at the time he speaks it, and thus the Thought Form is much clearer than it would be otherwise for the reason that he concentrates a great deal more attention upon it than he would ordinarily.

When the practitioner of the art gazes in a vessel, projecting in that his intentions against the person, or if he looks at the portrait of the person and pronounces his doom, he is concentrating a great deal more attention than he would ordinarily do, therefore he is making a clearer picture and one which will more greatly influence.

Curses are another form of Black Magic, inasmuch as they speed forth a certain condemnation, a certain doom, but they are efficacious only in the degree that they help in forming a mental picture, resulting in a Thought Form, of the doom which is to take place. A curse would impart no injury to the cursed party were it not for the Thought Form generated by the attitude of mind back of the curse, but the speaking of the curse enables one to express a much clearer picture than the average man would be able to do without use of some formula.

If you strike the picture of a person, an image of him, or anything of that kind while pronouncing a curse, it merely helps to emphasize your own state of mind. Your own state of consciousness is punctuated, as it were, by the act. Thus the Thought Form is made much more vivid than it would be otherwise, consequently it exercises a greater power in the work. Sometimes a lock of the person's hair or a picture of him, an article which he has had—anything of that kind may be thrown into the fire and, while it is being burned, the mind is concentrated upon the doom of the person and thus this act helps in the formation of the Mental picture, resulting in the destruction of the victim.

Another method is to take a piece of paper, parchment, and write on it the name of the victim, and then subject it to whatever inconvenience you wish to subject the person to. It helps you to concentrate on his name and as the name is very closely allied to the man, is, in fact, essentially a part of him, by concentrating upon the name, you bring the calamity on him because you are sending there the Thought Form that brings about the influence. You may burn up the parchment containing his name, at the same time imagining him in this burning condition, imagining him as burning, and this Thought Form will bring about this result; or you may put it in a poison solution, and as this becomes poisoned, so shall his being be poisoned, and in this way the terrible doom will be carried out. It is for this reason that the Chinese and quite a number of other nations do not like to give their names, and will under no consideration, have their pictures made; will not allow a photographer to photograph them, and the objections of Indians to being photographed is undoubtedly due to a fear that the photograph will be used for the purpose of practicing Black Magic upon them.

It may be said, in a general way, that Black Magic consists in the use of any formula or ceremony, any symbol or figure for the purpose of assisting the mind in the generation of a Thought Form detrimental to the life, health, wealth or happiness of a victim, and is of value only so far as it assists in the generation of the Thought Form. It may also be used for purposes of seduction. There is a man of considerable prominence, residing in the City of Chicago who has, by the use of Black Magic, succeeded in seducing a number of married women. The method is to get as near the person as possible; get in the same house, if possible; if not, do the best he can and make a symbol on the door—a cross or anything of the kind, to aid in the concentration, and will for the person to come to you. There are persons in possession of a sufficient degree of will, while making these symbols and concentrating, forming a picture of the person coming, to actually compel a woman to leave her bed and go to the person and return to her own house and the next morning know absolutely nothing of what transpired in the night. In such case it is a means of hypnotism and a very powerful one. Sometimes people will get up and go, acting under a powerful impulse that they cannot resist or understand, but will come to themselves before it is too late; otherwise, quite a great deal of vice is practiced in this way.

The use of all symbolic figures, ciphers and everything of that description is a means of fixing the picture, of generating the Thought Form and in this way bringing to bear those influences necessary to accomplish the result. Of course, when it is intended to invoke Devas in this way, it becomes Ceremonial Magic, but if it be merely in order to generate Thought Forms for the purpose of accomplishing evil, it is then within the realm of Black Magic.

This art should never be practiced, no matter what one's principles may be. Be he ever so infamous a villain he can not afford to practice Black Magic. You remember the old adage that bad wishes are like chickens, they always come home to roost; and this is true of malicious Thought Forms. They are sent forth and in many instances they destroy, but if they do not succeed in accomplishing their purpose, if they fail in the object for which they are sent forth, the affinity exists between them and the one who generated them; thus they rebound, like the veritable boomerang; they come back to the one who sent them—the chickens come home to roost, and thus he must receive the fruit of his practice when that practice is no longer efficacious.

Again, when the Thought Form has succeeded in destroying the victim it has no longer anything to do; it must be active, and inasmuch as it was directed against a particular individual, not against humanity in general, it does not go on and hunt other victims; it has accomplished its work; it returns to the one who sent it, and all the Thought Forms sent out by him, that have accomplished their purpose come back upon him. He is thus crushed to death by the rebound of the forces he has sent forth.

The life of the Black Magus never lasts very long. Fifteen or twenty years is as long as any of them can live. One who is not a Master will not live anything like as long as that. Also in many instances, they become insane, due to the terrible strain brought upon them. No person can practice this art without the greatest danger to himself every moment of his life and not only to himself, but to those connected with him by ties of love or friendship, association and everything of that kind, because if he is so positive that the Thought Form when it comes back can not injure him, can not penetrate his positive Aura, it will then go to the one nearest to him, the one most in sympathy with him, and in this way will strike the nearest victim to him, possible. For this reason, the Black Magus should never have any friends. If he has, he is simply exposing them to the rebound of the Thought Forms he has sent forth. He should never have any family, any relations, any associates, because every tie, every affinity existing between him and another is pointing that one to the doom coming from the rebound. The practice of so many Black Magi in living alone, in knowing no one, having no associates is, therefore, an act of benevolence in a way, because they are taking the chances themselves and not coming into that connection with mankind which will naturally open the way for the inroads of those terrible forces. Where the Black Magus associates with people, makes friends, lives in the house with other people, goes into society, it is for the specific purpose of surrounding himself with a number of decoys who will be the victims of the rebound. Catching these Thought Forms, they will consequently shelter him from the result of his evil deeds, because if the Thought Form finds it very difficult to penetrate his Aura, it will next seek a vcitim as near him as possible, one whose Aura will not present such difficulties. In this way he may escape, by causing others to suffer in his stead.

If you have the slightest idea that a man or woman is practicing Black Magic, whatever you do, do not associate with him or her. Do not have any feeling of sympathy for such a person. Have no mercy on the practitioner of Black Magic. Do not permit yourself to love him or think well of him at all. Realize fully the infamy of his character and, realizing this, do not countenance him for one moment. If you succeed in maintaining this attitude of absolute non-sympathy with the Black Magus you will be tolerably free from the rebound, but woe betide the man or woman who makes the Black Magus a friend, to find that sooner or later the positive force of the Magus is broken down, his spiritual power is sapped away, his force is gone and he weakens, permitting the Thought Forms which he has generated, to devour him. He is thus destroyed by the very forces he has generated. The path of the Shadow is ever the left hand, ever leading to destruction not to construction, and he who destroys others must himself, sooner or later be destroyed by the forces he has generated.

LESSON VI

BLACK ART

Black Art deals with the formation of Incubi and Succubi and is, perhaps, the most infamous of all the branches of art Magic.

Little is known of the Incubi and Succubi at the present time, but they are among the most terrible of all the beings known to the students of Magic. Paracelsus deals quite extensively with them in some of his hermetic works.

Briefly speaking, an Incubus is a male artificial elemental, generated through lust while a Succubus is the same, only female. What we mean is that the action of lust in men generates a number of artificial elementals termed Incubi whose very nature is lust, and lust on the part of women generates a number of feminine elementals whose nature is lust pure and simple. As the mind is dwelling on the sensual, the licentious, it generates a Thought Form which is in the nature of lust though this Thought Form is rather slight because the mind does not generate so much force when dwelling upon lust as does the Desire Nature, lust itself being an Astral activity and setting free a quantity of Astral force which is lustful and which gathers around the thought and forms for it an Astral Body, thus enabling this thought of lust to operate as an elemental on the Astral Plane. When the lust has descended to the Etheric region there is set free a quantity of Sperma, the Etheric counterpart of the sexual fluids, which forms the Etheric Double. We

(53)

have here, then, an elemental possessing mind, a powerful Astral body and an Etheric Double, and inasmuch as
this being is generated through the activity of lust, his
only desire is one of lust; that is to say, the only desire
of which he is capable is one of a sensual character. He
is fundamentally vicious in the sexual sense. His very
nature prompts him to search for everything which will
have the effect of gratifying his sensual appetite; his
mind dwells on the sensual and vicious only, being only
sexually active. He is in the very nature of things a
sex pervert, having no other nature, his nature being the
crystallization of sexual desire on the part of man, if he
be an Incubus, because it is man's desire for gratification that generates the Incubus.

On the other hand, if it be a Succubus, generated from
the desire, the lust of woman, its nature is equally sensual, equally given to lust, but its whole desire runs
after men.

What we must bear in mind is that each one of these
beings is an intelligent entity possessed of an overpowering desire—a Lust Elemental; not simply an abstract
principle, not simply a force in nature, but a being who
has no character save and except one of lust.

These beings are generated whenever the carnal desires of men or women are active. Not a moment do we
give way to sensual thoughts and desires but what we
are generating vast multitudes of these beings and peopling the world about us with them. Inasmuch as their
nature is positively and exclusively given to lust, they
naturally undertake to gratify it, and, strange as it may
seem, they do not secure this gratification by intercourse
with each other, but the Incubus must attach himself to
the Aura of some woman and by sapping away her magnetic principle, by exciting in her carnal desire and thus

causing the outflow of the sex principle, he may get satisfaction. Likewise, the Succubus must attach herself to the Aura of a man and by exciting sexual impulses and causing the outflow of the sex principle in him, secure satisfaction. It is really a process of seduction that is going on, and whenever a woman gives way to lustful desires, she is generating thousands of seducers of the male sex; likewise, when man gives way to lust he may know that he is generating thousands of seducers of the female sex. This process of seduction must go on *ad infinitum* as long as the two sexes give way to lust, thus generating seducing sex elementals. If people would only realize this they would surely abstain from much of their carnal desire, but unfortunately, they do not realize the terrible consequences to come from their indulgence of the sexual vice.

These elementals can remain on the physical plane and thus act upon the Auras of people only by reason of their Etheric Doubles which are formed of the sperma generated in the human organism by reason of the lust which is there awakened. It naturally follows that they are very anxious to perpetuate the Etheric Double, but the Double must become exhausted in time and, in fact it can last only a few days. In a few days it becomes exhausted and unless it can be replenished in some way, reproduced, they will be unable to continue on the physical plane. They will have to withdraw to the Astral Plane. But that is not all. Unless they secure Astral matter their Astral bodies will, in time disintegrate; their entire principles must sooner or later disintegrate. It is, therefore, absolutely essential if they would perpetuate their existence, that they have the substance of which their Astrals are formed, this Astral Desire stuff, by means of which they may perpetuate their existence.

This is to be secured only by awakening desire in man or woman as the case may be, and when this substance of the Astral Body is thrown off, instead of allowing it to become an artificial elemental, draw this substance to themselves into their own bodies and organize it into their own substance. Likewise, they draw the Manas of the impure thought into their Mental Bodies and reproduce themselves. Their lives are, therefore, dependent upon the lust in men or women. They must, consequently awaken the lust principle, put a person in a state of lust in order to get the substance for rebuilding their bodies, their nourishment being derived in that way. Consequently, we find there are two motives for this influence which they exercise. The Incubi stimulate the lust of men in order that they may get the substance to replenish their bodies, and they also stimulate the lust principle in women to secure the sexual gratification which they find in the sex principle of the woman. The Succubi on the contrary, stimulate the lust principle of woman to gain the substance for the reproduction of their bodies and that of man to secure the gratification which gives them pleasure, that for which they have a powerful propensity.

Understand, the only pleasure in life for a sex elemental, is in the sensation that comes to them by reason of their connection with the sex principle in a human being of the opposite sex, consequently their whole nature runs after it. They have an overpowering appetite for the sex principle of the opposite sex in the human and draw to them that of their own sex in order that they may continue to live. Every time a man or woman gives way to carnal desire or carnal thought he or she is developing thousands of these elementals. Not only is this true, but when the sex fluids are discharged elementals take up the substance as it evaporates, gathering up the etheric part and making use of it for the purpose of restoring their etheric bodies so that they can continue on the physical plane. They excite the sex instinct in boys and young men, literally driving them to commit masturbation in order that they may secure the seminal fluid to use in this way. Every person who has fallen into that vice has experienced great difficulty in avoiding the practice. The impulse comes upon him so strong that he can not resist it, and do whatever he will, he finds that he must commit the act. As a matter of fact, he is not responsible. He is being attacked by the Incubi who are forcing him to supply them with the material for the rebuilding of their etheric doubles. In the same way when a girl or woman yields to an uncontrollable impulse to practice self abuse she is yielding to the suggestion, the hypnotic influence of the Succubi who are thus driving her to supply them with material for the replenishing of their etheric bodies.

The great sin in masturbation, therefore, is not so much the evil effect it has on the person practicing the act as it is in the supplying of the Incubi and Succubi with the element necessary to reproduce their physical bodies, thus enabling them to continue on the physical plane and stimulate the sex passion in others so that they will, in turn, be driven to the same vice. There is nothing, therefore, so abominable as the practice of self abuse, not because of the bad effect it has on the one who is doing it, but because of the terrible swarm of evil entities that are being generated through the activity of this lust principle. The reason the Bible curses the man who shall spill his seed on the ground is not so much on account of its effect on him or because he is depriving himself of seed as because the very act will cause the germination of myriads of entities and will supply them with physical bodies; will also enable other entities of the same class to secure physical bodies. The Law of Moses required a man if he had a nocturnal emission to immediately get up and wash because in this way the evaporation of the seminal fluid was prevented and, therefore, the generation of elementals from it became impossible.

When Christ says "Whosoever shall look upon a woman to lust after her hath committed adultery with her already in his heart" he refers to the same terrible consequences of lust, for if either a man or a woman lusts he or she is, by reason of that emotion generating these elementals; but if a man lusts after a particular woman all the Incubi that he generates during that act of lust will, in their nature have a propensity driving them in her direction. They will have the same lust for her that he had while he was generating them. The result will be every one of those elementals will be infatuated with that woman; will attach themselves to her Aura and will seek gratification of their propensity by exciting the sexual impulse in her, thus sapping away her sex energy. To lust after a woman is, therefore, to produce a swarm of Incubi having the one aim in life of seducing that woman. There is, therefore, no crime in the calendar half so infamous as lusting after a woman. In its very nature it is generating these elementals who will go to her; therefore, it will have the tendency to compel her to become sexually guilty. The elementals are so many warriors attacking the citadel of her virtue, therefore, it is an act of seduction in every way; in fact, it partakes very closely of the nature of rape for a person to do anything of the kind. The converse is true of a woman who lusts after a man. The Succubi are thus generated, having this strong desire for gratification.

These Incubi and Succubi generated through lust after a particular man or woman are never satisfied with anyone else, but insist upon having that particular man or woman. That is why lusting after a person is such an infamous crime.

The practice of Black Art is for the definite purpose of generating these artificial elementals. The art is gone through with for no other purpose than the generation of Incubi and Succubi. In certain rites among the Bacchian Mystics and the Simonian and certain of the more corrupt Gnostics debauchery was resorted to for the purpose of generating these elementals.

It is hard to believe, nevertheless it is true that the Bacchanalian orgies were not simply to gratify the lust of the people, for many of them did not have so very much lust themselves. They were for the purpose of generating artificial elementals, and the Bacchanalian revels were gone through with in order to set free this desire principle and generate millions of those Incubi and Succubi. In certain instances considerable quantities of the sex fluid was employed to provide bodies for the elementals. The elementals gathered there at those revels and reproduced their bodies.

It may be asked why people should resort to such vices. We know from the writings of the fathers that Simon Magus and his sect resorted to this practice. Now, why is it they did it. Obviously for this reason: The Incubi and Succubi know they owe their existence to the person who generated them and also if he will continue to reproduce them, to provide them with the means of replenishing their being, they are quite ready to serve him, to do his bidding, particularly as they desire only sexual gratification. They thus become serv-

ants of the one who generates them, particularly if he
generates them deliberately knowing what he is doing.
There is a tie between them. Consequently, the practitioner of the Black Art is able to generate millions of
elementals who will do his bidding. They are under the
control of his will and can be sent against whoever he
sees fit. If there is a woman whose virtue he wants to
violate all he has to do is to send a sufficient number of
Incubi to attack her until she is debauched by the Incubi;
then in time the citadel of her virtue is broken down and
she will submit to abuse at the hand of man. Thus he
may be able to seduce the purest virgins for his own use
or for the sake of others. In this way women are prepared for the brothel and for the positions of kept mis-
tresses and everything of that kind.

The time was when it was known that there were people who could do these things and if some scoundrel
wanted to overcome the virtue of a woman he went and
employed a practitioner of the Black Art to arrange the
business for him. Fortunately, however, there is not
so much faith at the present time in their ability to do
these things; but the black artist has a particular spite
at sexual virtue; he cannot endure the idea of people
being pure and he is at war with virtue. He generates
these beings for the purpose of overcoming virtue. Also
he knows that it is the sex principle which enables a
person to become self centered, positive, powerful. People are easily made his dupes whenever their sex force
is dissipated. He will, therefore, seduce them in this
way, cause their sex principle to be sapped away in order
that they may be weakened, lose their fighting force so
that he may the more easily be enabled to sap away their
other powers and get control of them in other ways.

Black Art is, therefore, employed as a means of

weakening the victim so that he or she will be unable to resist the magical force along other lines; will become a victim of whatever force may be directed against him and in this way the door is opened for all the vices of the dark magi.

Black Art, bear in mind, is only that state of magic where the sexual vices are resorted to for the purpose of generating artificial elementals. When a person, otherwise pure, commits sexual vices in order to generate the Incubi and Succubi or to provide those already generated with bodies in order that he may control them and send them against a definite person, he is practicing Black Art.

All the religions where sexual vice is resorted to in certain dark rites are based upon Black Art. They generate the Incubi and Succubi in order that they may be employed for the perpetuation of works of Magic as a means unto the accomplishment of the Black Art. It is not, therefore, merely sex vice, but vice practiced for a definite purpose, when the sexual desire is not there, for the black artist at other times is relatively pure.

LESSON VII

SORCERY

Sorcery really consists in the acting through the principle which is known among the students of Magic as Mumia, and this Mumia is really the substance of the Etheric Double, which is present in some part of the being after it has been removed, for instance, the parings of the finger nails and the toe nails, the hair cut from the head, skin, or a part of the flesh, a limb or anything of that kind after it has been removed from the body. This is also true in the case of excrement or anything of that kind, the perspiration—everything that contains within it the Etheric principle of the person from whom it came. And, now, the rationale of Mumia is to act upon this in such a way as to affect the ether which is within the body, so that by acting upon this Mumia you can act upon the man himself. This is the purpose of Sorcery.

Now, we must first establish the fact that by acting upon the Mumia you can act upon the Etheric Double of the subject from which the Mumia was derived. For instance, there was a case of a man who had a leg amputated, and this leg was put in a coffin and nailed up; a nail being driven through the coffin into it, penetrated the leg, but nobody knew anything about it. The man continually kept complaining of a pain in his leg, saying they had driven a hole through his leg, and insisted that they should go and take up his leg and pull the nail out. They opened the box and, sure enough, the nail was there;

they pulled it out and he never had any more trouble with his leg. All this shows that there was a connection between the leg and the man from whom it was severed. The explanation of Mumia accounts for this quite satisfactorily. It states the Etheric Principle was in the leg, and that it was also in the man, and there was a vibratory harmony between the two. He, therefore, felt, became conscious of the action upon the leg. Now, unless there has been such a severe shock to a limb—a crushing or something of that kind—so that sensation is impossible, this condition will last until the leg has been entirely disorganized.

Again, there is a case which is given quite at length by Professor Fowler. In this case a leg was cut off and experimented on. They had the man's leg on the floor above where he was—in the upper room in the hospital, and would stick pins in it; and every time they stuck a pin in it, the man would cry out. They put it close to the fire, and he would complain that his leg was being scorched, proving that there was a vibratory communication, between the Etheric Principle in him and the Etheric Principle in his leg. Although it had been severed and was several feet distant, yet this communication was going on between the Etheric Principle in the leg and the Etheric Principle in his body.

There have even been cases of grafting of skin from the face of one person to that of another. In many instances when the man from whom the skin was taken died, the grafted skin began to rot, and the skin rotted wherever it was. When he died, that Etheric Principle disintegrated and brought about the decay. There are cases where this does not take place. It is no contradiction, however. The reason is, that in those cases where the grafting of the skin is permanent, the person from

whom the skin was taken has lived several years after
it was taken off, so in the course of time the Mumia was
changed. Consequently the change is brought about—
it is completely transformed. But in every instance
where the system has not had time to change the vibration and bring it completely into a state of identification
with its own Etheric Principle, this rotting, etc., has
taken place.

Now, Paracelsus, by medicating the blood which had
been taken from a man's veins and which was placed in
a bottle, cured blood poison on a number of occasions.
The only way in which this could be done, therefore, was
to act upon the Ether contained in that blood. He has,
also, taken a lock of hair cut from a man's head, treated
it, and cured a headache in the man from whom the lock
of hair was taken. A psychometrist can take a lock of
your hair, and tell your character, diagnose your disease and everything of that kind. It is the Mumia contained in the hair. Now, Sorcery is the use of this principle, not accidentally, but systematically for the express
purpose of acting upon the Etheric Principle within the
body of a person, and it involves the idea, to a great extent, of selfishness. It is not absolutely necessary that
it should be evil—but it is usually of an evil or selfish
character. It is to act upon this principle within the
person.

Now, remember, if you act upon the Etheric Double,
as the Etheric Double is the force which forms and gives
expression to the gross physical body, you can, in this
way, act directly upon the principle of the patient, or
the subject of your practice. You act directly upon his
body whenever you act upon his Etheric Principle, and
thus the physical power is brought under your control,
and you may, also to a certain extent, affect the Astral.

Now, by Sorcery, the mind is not influenced; the feelings may be, to a certain extent, and absolutely, the physical. It is, in fact, the physical mainly, that is aimed at by the practice of Sorcery. The sorcerer will secure, if possible, a lock of your hair, or something containing your Etheric Principle—something containing your Mumia, and he will then go to work in this way, and, by acting upon it and keeping his mind always fixed upon you at the same time he will establish a certain impression on the object, whatever it may be. He will impress something on the Etheric Principle, on that Mumia, and he will project this to you by mental picturing, imagery, etc., so that it will have the effect upon your Etheric Principle. Remember, by establishing this sensation, or this influence upon that Etheric Principle, that Mumia, and at the same time thinking of that as being you and thinking "I am doing this to this particular person" the sorcerer is able to exercise tremendous influence; the influence that he will exercise is simply awful, when he works in this way, striving for the accomplishment of certain ends.

Now, if the sorcerer cannot get any part of you, he will employ some article on the same principle that the psychometrist works—taking an article which you have handled, in order to ascertain your internal condition; but the sorcerer takes this article in order to establish certain relations within your being, by acting upon your Etheric Principle through this Mumia. Also, a person may use this principle for the working of positive evil. He may, for instance, take Mumia containing a disease, and if he wants to cure a person and has no particular solicitude for the welfare of anybody else, he will take anything containing this person's Mumia and put it in a package so that if anyone takes it up and opens it, with his suggestion as he put it in there, holding the thought, that one will take on the disease. The very moment he takes this package up, he takes on the disease of this patient, and thus the disease will leave this person. If you impress it on this Mumia in this way, the result will be that whenever it comes into the hands of a person, though he be perfectly well, it will come into contact with his own Etheric Principle and will establish the vibration of that disease, and the vibration will leave the person who has been sick, the person who has taken up the package receiving it.

This is a method of treatment which is even advised in the works of Albertus Magnus. He was a catholic bishop, and gave treatment in this way to over one-quarter of those he treated. He placed the Mumia in the road so that people would walk over it, and the first person who came into contact with it would be immediately affected through his Etheric Principle, and thus the disease would be transferred to him. You may plant the Mumia under somebody's house, for instance, and it will have the effect of making the whole family sick with disease. This is practiced to a great extent, by people not realizing what they are doing.

We used to know some people in the South who firmly believed that if you had a sty on your eye, for instance, you could go to a crossing of two roads and stand there and say, "Sty, sty, get off my eye, and fall on the first one's eye that passes by," firmly believing it, and it would if there were sufficient force of imagination there and suggestion. You cause the Etheric Principle to leave your being and especially of that eye to pass into the ground there so that the ground becomes charged with it, and thus becomes Mumia; and the first person stepping over it stands in great danger of its affecting him; because those transferences have taken place a number of times people continue to believe in those superstitions. Wherever superstitions are held it absolutely indicates the continuance of the occurrences of the thing involved.

Also, you may even make use of disease Mumia out of pure revenge, if you want to impress a disease upon a person or a number of persons, Mumia may be used in this way. You may write a letter, for instance, and while you are writing it you may impress your hands upon it magnetizing it, and at the same time impressing upon it the thought that a certain calamity will come to the person who receives it; and by this you will set up a vibration upon the Mumia of the person, and if he don't know how to prevent it you will very likely bring about the calamity which you have in mind. As a matter of fact, the danger of infection from contagious diseases through the mails is simply a case of Mumia acting upon the Etheric Principle of the person who receives the letter. The infection from clothes is in reality through this Etheric Principle which is operating along all those lines.

You may also, act upon a person's Etheric Principle by any Mumia. It makes no difference whether it is his or not, you can get control of it to a certain extent through any Mumia. Of course, another's Mumia will not have the effect that his own would; but if you get hold of any kind of Mumia you can, to a certain extent, be able to influence the person, and anything you do to that, the same effect will be produced upon him; sticking pins into it will have precisely the very same effect; burnnig, cutting, bruising, no matter what it is, it will have that same effect. And this is the reason why sorcerers rob graves; it is to get corpses, so that before they have disintegrated, just as soon as they are buried they get the corpses out for they contain the Mumia, the Etheric Principle. Now, by concentration of mind, they establish a connection between vibration en rapport between this Etheric Principle contained in this dead body and the Etheric Principle contained in the organism of the victim; and having established this rapport, you go to work on this body and if you want to, injure him physically and accomplish these injuries. If you don't want to do this, you go to work and, having established this connection, proceed to hypnotize this corpse and tell it what you want to do; and by going to work on this corpse soon you govern the rate of vibration, the circulation of its Etheric Principle—because, remember, the Etheric Double does not leave the gross body until such a time as the gross body has been entirely disintegrated. Now, as the gross body is permeated by the Etheric Principle, you make it move and vibrate according to your will, so that you form the mental pictures at will, and accomplish those results. You have already established the connection between it and the Etheric Double in your victim. In this way you will be able to govern and direct the Etheric Double of your victim. Consequently you can get control of his physical. What is the result? By getting control of the Etheric Double you can make his physical nature control him in any way you want it to.

You have all heard of the stories of the witches and sorcerers robbing graves to get corpses, and even taking them and dividing them when there was not enough to go around, one taking one piece and another taking another. They wanted to use this Mumia, and thus get control of the Etheric Principle of their victims. And if they can do this they can accomplish their purposes whatever they may be.

Now, it was owing to this fact that cremation was developed. You will find this custom of cremation among those people where a considerable bit of magic, considerable occultism was practiced. By cremation the body has not the Etheric Double, the Etheric Double thus being separated nad escaping, and then this body could not be used as a means of performing works of sorcery. And it was really on this account that cremation was established, thereby making sorcery impossible. In those nations where they did not have this fear of sorcery, it was not practiced; among the Egyptians sorcery was never practiced. They practiced a lot of magic, which was not always the best; they practiced more black art, but not sorcery, and, therefore, no cremation was heard of in Egypt. Now, we find that cremation was resorted to in order to prevent the commission of sorcery; and when you stop and consider the vast extent of territory over which cremation is a custom, you can then realize the importance of sorcery in the past. All the bodies which are taken out of graves are not taken out for the use of doctors alone; quite a number of bodies are stolen for the purpose of performing works of sorcery, getting control of some one's Etheric Double and, therefore, accomplishing its work. Now, when we realize the use to which bodies have been subjected, we can see the depths to which the sorcerer will stoop in order to accomplish her or his purpose. A great many of the sorcerers and sorceresses in India, for instance, live in the cemeteries, and in all the eastern countries they live in the tombs and around there among the graves; and a great many people have asked the reason why they have done this, why they have lived among them. By living there they can even get in that close touch with the bodies while they are still in the graves, and they may even call out the Etheric Double for a short space of time, out of the body, out of the coffin, making it come out to the top of the ground if they have sufficient force, and then bringing it into this connection with the one whom they wish to influence, they begin to act upon it in the same way. It is really at the bottom of stories about the ghouls who stay in the graveyards and feed on the corpses. They draw forth the Etheric Principle, and direct and influence.

Sorcery, then, is the acting upon the Etheric Principle, either that of the victim or of another, for the purpose of gaining control of the victim, or of doing him an injury, or of throwing on him some condition; no matter what the purpose in doing this may be, it is always injurious to some one. It is different from White Magic; you can really benefit some one without doing any one harm by using White Magic.

The Etheric Principle is, in many instances, found to permeate whatever has been handled or worn or used by the party or person, even after his death. It is to prevent sorcery that most of those nations where cremation was universally applied among the ancients, have adopted the custom of burning on the funeral pyre everything, all the personal effects of the deceased, destroying his weapons and everything of that kind. All his personal effects are destroyed, because there will be Mumia by which something evil may be accomplished. And the modern practice of destroying everything of those who die of consumption is really an application of the same principle. It is Mumia in that case. We all recognize the truth of Mumia when applied to physical ailments, contagious diseases, but when the same principle is applied to the occult side of things, most of us cannot realize anything reasonable in it. It is just as true in its application to occultism as it is in its application to the physical relations of things. Sorcery has, therefore, an absolute physical basis, the Etheric Principle, and the fact that it continues to be the same, having the same rate of vibration, is precisely the same if that principle which contains it has been removed from the earth, as it was before, and in death it does not change. The further fact that this may be acted upon, that it is possible to get control of it, or to produce certain effects upon this Etheric Principle, and by bringing that into connection, into vibratory harmony with the Etheric Principle in a living man or woman, to cause that condition or that vibration, that condition of this Mumia to be transferred to it, the Etheric Double of the living person, and thus to establish that condition in his own Etheric Principle, and by gradually bringing down to a lower state of vibration, to produce the same effect upon his gross physical body.

Therefore, to produce death or life, or to produce any kind of disease or to get control of a person, all those practices are made perfectly possible, and perfectly convenient, by getting control of the Etheric Principle and acting on that through this Mumia, thus transferring it to the Etheric Principle within the body of the person, or, rather, victim.

LESSON VIII.

NECROMANCY.

Necromancy consists in the use made of the Mumia resident in dead bodies, or in the calling up of the Etheric Principle in those who are dead, from the graves, etc. The Mumia has the same character after death that it had before. It is an impression of the mind, heart, etc., upon this substance, a kind of Etheric Brain. Possessing this Etheric Brain it consequently preserves an impression of the past thinking and feeling. It contains within itself, in fact, the entire past life from the moment life has begun until the point of death. This is preserved not in the form of a thinking mind, but simply as an impression, a copy, a duplicate; thus we can read the Etheric Double as a record of what has been passed through so far as there was a memory of it at the time of death. All that was in the mind and heart; all, in fact, that existed in the memory at the moment of dissolution, continues in the Etheric Memory and when man dies the Etheric Double remains in connection with his gross physical body until that is entirely dissolved; until the last particle of the skeleton is decayed. When this has taken place, the body having entirely decayed, the Etheric Double then has no longer an abiding place; it must enter the Etheric Realm, the eighth sphere where in time it will disintegrate; but it continues until the destruction of the gross body, no matter how long that may be.

Necromancy is the art by which these Etheric bodies

are called up from the physical, are separated from the physical, caused to come out and thus, in this abstracted condition, they may be interrogated in regard to what was in that man's past life in regard to what was in his memory at that time. It is this principle that is really operative in the invocation and worship of the names of the dead; by calling up by certain ceremonies an Etheric Body or Shade, we may interrogate it, not that it has the consciousness or capacity to speak and answer us, but rather that we are able to unite our Etheric Double with the Shade so that they become perfectly blended and thus that impression is brought into our consciousness, that vibration is sensed, and, by the union with the Etheric Principle, we know what was in the consciousness of the man at the time of his death.

Necromancy is, therefore, a means of acquiring knowledge regarding the past life and consciousness of a given individual. We may make whatever use of that knowledge we see fit, but by invoking the Shade we can come to a recognition of that which was in his consciousness at the time of such invocation.

Not only is it possible for us to pry into the secrets of the dead, but we may also, by charging this Shade with a sufficient amount of our force, send it to a person, make it appear to him, and as it is the Shade of a dead person, it will assume his form, and thus we can send a first class spirit apparition to a live person. These apparitions may give them commands, require them to do certain things, and the authority of the dead may thus be employed for whatever we have in mind.

Necromancy does not relate to the use we make of this power. Necromancy *per se* is the calling up of the Shade, and whatever application we may make of this power, it is still Necromancy. We may use it from a motive relatively good—although all Necromancy is evil—or we may use it from the most vicious motives. But the essence of Necromancy is in the act of calling up the Shade. The Shade may, as we say, be sent to persons in different parts of the world, appearing that way, becoming the embodiment of that person's past, as it were, appearing to his friends, imposing upon their credulity and making them do things which they would not ordinarily do. It may, also, be sent, having first had impressed upon it a definite order, a definite command, and thus be induced to afflict a person by causing a disturbance in his Etheric Principle, acting in the same way that the Etheric Double of a living person will act in the practice of Witchcraft.

It may also be used as the vehicle for an Astral Body to go forth, impersonating himself as another object. Those practitioners of Magic who dwell in the tombs, among the dead, who remain around graveyards are practicing Necromancy. They remain there for the purpose of calling up the Shades, consulting with them, forcing them to do certain things which they would not do without such invocation. In fact, they have no capacity to do anything. A Shade is simply a shade, not a being in himself, and can act only as he is directed by the Intelligence; however, when so directed he can impress upon the consciousness of those with whom he comes in contact what is already established in his Etheric Brain, that is, in the memory. Wherever the dead are so invoked from the graves, it is for one of these purposes.

The offering of blood in the sacrifices of the heathens was for the purpose of giving strength to the Shades, in order that they might replenish their bodies, getting the physical energy from the blood, also drawing it from the life and the Astral principle that the animal soul contains; thus they would be able to attain a certain measure of vitality and emotional activity. When they continue to replenish their being, thus to live indefinitely, owing to this influence, it becomes possible for them to do a great many things they would not be able to do otherwise.

The offering of human sacrifices to the dead, the watering of the graves of certain persons with the blood of the victims, is really for the purpose of giving that Shade renewed physical force, life and Astral matter in order that it may continue its life; that it may continue to commit the depredations which appeal to it and to do all the evil possible to those Shades.

It is the purpose of the Creator that disintegration should take place; that the Shades should die, should cease to be as the body gradually returns to the dust from whence it came; thus the Shade will disintegrate. It is, therefore, an impious interference with the decree of the Almighty, when one perpetuates the existence of the Shade. But those Shades will serve anyone who will give them the means of perpetuating their existence, and the poetry of Greece and Rome, wherever it speaks of the sacrifices of blood being offered to them, or the worship of the Manes of the dead, is recognizing this fundamental principle. It is for this reason that the Greeks always recognized those beings as abiding in Hades, the underworld, the place of death, and why is Hades the underworld? Because it is under the ground; that is, it is under the sense of being within the world; it is in the Etheric Principle of the earth that the abode of the Shades is to be found after the body is decayed, after it has ceased to be a suitable vehicle for the perpetuation of the Shade.

Cremation was really designed for the purpose of preventing the invocation of the Shades. By cremation, the body is destroyed. In this way the vehicle ceases and the Shade disintegrates in a comparatively short time.

Again, we find that in those countries where cremation is practiced Magic is quite common. It, therefore, follows that it was out of their experience with Necromancy that the people developed the idea of cremation. Cremation is really a preventive measure. In those countries where there has been no such practice, we find that cremation has never been resorted to. Among the Jews and the Christian nations, where the people in general do not resort to those practices, where very little of the practice of magic has occurred to disgrace the history of the world, cremation is regarded as decidedly improper. The Egyptians, on the other hand, embalm their dead in order that they may be preserved, and the dead are embalmed in order to provide a home for the Etheric Double in order that it may continue, for the Egyptians, believing in the resurrection and holding the idea that man must have all his principles preserved and they must all be reunited, when, in the true sense it is not the resurrection, but rather a revival—consequently they wanted to preserve the Etheric Double intact, as well as the body, so that the different principles of the being would come together, the sideral body or what we term the Astral Body, the Mind or Manas, the Soul, the Spirit, the Life Principle and the Name, all uniting with the Double or Shade and the Gross Body, they would again begin their existence. But a number of Egyptians got to regarding the Etheric Double as something worthy of worship and honor, so that in the course of time Necromancy began to be practiced among them. We find that even among the Jews there were some who practiced Necromancy, calling up the dead, and it was this practice that was so severely punishēd by the Jewish Law, under the name of Necromancy. Whoever might call up the dead was to be punished with death, without mercy in any single instance. It was because of this nefarious practice, because of the terrible consequences it had for those who were the victims and also for the ones who made use of the Shades, because sooner or later they would bring themselves into bondage to them, because it should be borne in mind that the Shade can be consulted only by uniting it and blending it with your own Etheric Body. The result of such blending is the total extinction of the higher principles so far as their activity is concerned and the abnormal development of the Etheric Double. In the course of time it becomes so developed that it is out of all proportion to the higher principles, and leaves them in the shade, so to speak; also getting out of proportion to the Gross body, in time it is projected, the separation between the Gross body and the Etheric Double becomes established and as this separation becomes more and more complete, as closer and closer we approach that state where the Etheric Double exists momentarily separate and apart from the body, we develop an existence independent of the Gross Body and at the same time a vibration very closely analogous to that of the Etheric Double of the dead—in other words, of the Shades; we are taking on the nature of the Shades by reason of our close connection with them, and we will finally establish such a state of sympathy that the Shade will be permanently separated from the Physical Body and will be drawn into the realm of Shades. This is what is meant by the Greek stories of the living souls' descent into Hades. When they have so descended, they are usually unable to return. Sometimes they can, but very often they are confined there.

We have stories in the Babylonian records, referring
to the same practice. The invocation of Samuel by the
Witch of Endor was not an invocation of his soul or
spirit and not even of his Astral Body; it was an act of
Necromancy; it was the calling up of his Shade, for we
have it positively stated that she asked Saul who he
would have "come up" not "come down" and he said
"Samuel." Then she says that she sees "men like gods,
coming up out of the earth." The whole story of the
raising of Samuel is a story of Necromancy, the raising
of a Shade, not the calling down of a spirit from above.

The nefarious practice of Necromancy is, therefore,
one of the most infamous of all the practices of a magical
character, and yet is resorted to quite often. Many of
the cases of the dead being raised out of their graves and
made to appear before the seance and answer certain
questions are really only cases of Necromancy and inasmuch as its consequence is the enslaving of the being,
the uniting of the Etheric Double and in many instances
the losing of the soul, so that the soul is separated from
the lower principles and so brought in bondage, and even
in some cases the bringing of the soul itself into bondage to the lower elements, holding it down in that state,
subjective to the dark realm of Hades, it becomes absolutely evident, therefore, that never should any person practice it.

Mediums who practice etherealization and materialization are also traveling along this devious path, for the
etherealized spirit is, in nine cases out of ten, nothing
but the Etheric Double of the medium and, by separat-
ing the Etheric Double from the Gross Body, the medium
is developing that state when this enslavement will become possible. The same is true in the case of materialization. Also when dealing with the Shades; when try-

ing to communicate with the dead; the great danger is that the medium will really call up the Shade of some dead one and unite her own Etheric Principle with it, and thus she is likely to come into bondage to the Shades. When some persons have been carried away by the Shades and their bodies have been found, this is really what has taken place. Therefore, our advice must at all times be in the most positive terms, whatever you do, have nothing to do with Necromancy. It means the death of the soul; it means the enslaving of all the higher powers, and the bringing of one's Etheric Principle into the Hadean realm; the sinking of one's being into the Eighth Sphere before the time comes for death, and in this case it does not separate the Etheric from the Astral; that is not what takes place as would be the case in the ordinary death, but unfortunately, the Astral is taken into the realm of death with the Etheric and thus, instead of going on to the Astral Plane, descends to the Eighth Sphere.

LESSON IX

WITCHCRAFT.

In its more restricted sense, Witchcraft is the art of afflicting the Etheric Double of the victim, not through any agent as in the previous forms of the Dark Art, but by the direct operation of the Etheric Principle of one's self; in other words, the Magnetic Body is temporarily separated from the Gross Body and, clothing the Astral and higher vehicles, is enabled to pass through space and afflict the Magnetic Body of the victim, even though it is in complete connection with the Gross Body, because the Astral is clothed with the Magnetic Body itself, therefore able to bring about certain effects in the Magnetic Body of the victim. They, being of the same substance, are interactive, and any disturbance that may be brought about in the Magnetic Body of the victim will react upon his Gross Body, and in this way bring about those physical disturbances that have attracted so much attention in the study of Witchcraft.

The history of the Witchcraft trials clearly brings to our attention the fact that it is quite possible for one who has become a Witch or a Warlock to separate the Magnetic Body from the Gross Body and, clothed with it, to travel to different parts of the world, over a considerable distance or else only a very short distance, and act upon the persons who are intended as victims.

Not only is this true, but the changing from the state of Etheric life to that in the Gross Body and vice versa may be accomplished instantaneously. No one who is not able to separate, with comparative ease, the Magnetic from the Gross Body, is able to follow the craft. It is the same mediumistic principle which we see operating in the materializing meduim that is employed in the practice of Witchcraft, only the materializing medium has the Etheric Body to go beyond the Gross Body without being personally conscious of what is taking place, while the Witch or Warlock is absolutely conscious and goes forth out of the body for this specific purpose.

The nocturnal visits to the places where the Witches and Warlocks met, were likewise cases of visits in the etheric form. Much sport has been created for the ignorant by the statements about going through the air, riding on broomsticks and everything of that kind. While, of course, there is a great deal of exaggeration as well as a great deal of nonsense connected with the stories, yet there can be no doubt that the Witches and Warlocks did meet, making their trips through the air, having separated from the Gross Bodies, and did assemble at places and celebrate their orgies; but, of course, much of the stories told was untrue.

The stories about pinching people, sticking pins in them, etc., are also perfectly rational when we realize that the mere picturing of the idea by the Etheric Double would create the same impression in that of another person and would thus react upon the body. Those terrible sufferings for which no physical cause could be assigned, were nothing more nor less than the afflictions of the Magnetic Body reacting upon the Gross Body.

Again, the stories about the Witches having their Imps are not untrue, but perfectly logical, perfectly rational, when we realize that the Elementals might very appropriately be attracted to them and might be employed as their agents, doing their bidding. We find that these

Elementals required, as the condition upon which they would work for the Witch or Warlock that they should be suckled, and they came in certain forms as birds or sometimes pigs, rats, toads, etc., and they were real Elementals that were kept by the Witches, not natural, but artificial Elementals. Their physical existence was, consequently, dependent upon their taking into their systems certain physical forces, either etheric or grossly physical. The habit of allowing them to suck different parts of the body, which developed the teats that were recognized as marks by the witch-finders, enabled them to draw blood from the body; likewise a great deal of ether, which enabled them to replenish their physical and etheric bodies. It was by this practice that the Imps maintained their existence; but in order to continue in this physical life they must, of course, have a patron, and to secure this patron they must do his or her bidding. Consequently they must do whatever the patron sent them forth to do. Witchcraft was, therefore, the means of providing employment for the Imps, and the sucking of the Witch maintained the life of the Imp. The Imp was dependent upon the Witch for physical existence, and the Witch was dependent upon the Imp's service for success in Witchcraft; that is, where she was not able to fully accomplish that work herself. It should be borne in mind that the Imps were employed by those who were not, in the higher sense of the words, successful Witches and Warlocks. The one who was able to go out in the Double at will did not depend upon the Imp and did not make use of him, but those not so highly developed had to make use of the Imps. The blood feud or union, generally represented by the signing in the devil's book, with one's own blood and receiving the devil's mark, really consisted in that harmony and coöperation which resulted in a blending of the Etheric Principle of the Witch with the spirit of an evil spirit, in this way establishing the union, so that they became one.

When the afflicted at Salem and other places recognized the apparitions of the Witches the truth is the Witch was really present in her Etheric Form and was recognized. The features were perfectly plain to those afflicted girls, who were really clairvoyants; and again when they appeared as someone else, taking the forms of other persons and impersonating innocent people, they did so by leaving their physical bodies and in this Etheric Form visualizing mentally, upon certain things, causing themselves to assume a definite form and thus becoming, for the time being, the duplicate of the person they wished to impersonate. In this way it is quite possible for one to pass himself off for an entirely different person. Likewise, if they wanted to represent animals, dogs and everything of that kind, they could do so, being in their Etheric Form, it being only necessary to form a vivid picture of what they were going to be and then they could assume this form and present themselves everywhere. Not only is it possible to do this, but one who has sufficient power of mental picturing, one who can form the picture with sufficient vividness and who at the same time has a very powerful Etheric Body, may materialize this form, so that his Etheric Double ceases to be etheric and really becomes a gross physical body. Stories of witches taking the form of animals and being wounded while in that form and then when they come back to their natural form retaining the wounds are too thoroughly attested to be doubted by anyone who is willing to accept the evidence, and at the same time they teach the great basic principles underlying this terrible phenomena of Witchcraft. A Witch has been known to turn herself into a dog, that is to bear the form of a dog—not simply etheric, but in a material form, and while retaining this form, to be wounded, to be bitten, and when she returned to her human shape, that is, when she entered the Gross Body, those wounds which were inflicted upon the Magnetic Body were impressed upon the gross physical body. This may be understood if we realize the fact of stigmata; by forming the picture in the mind continually of certain wounds, they will be inflicted on the body. Saint Theresa meditated upon Christ in her heart so much, Christ crucified and everything, that it was physically formed in her heart, and when an autopsy was performed on her at the time of her death, it was found that in her heart there was a miniature Christ crucified. Again, we have the case of Saint Francis, who, by reason of continually meditating upon the crucifixion of Christ, at last received the wounds of Christ, and there have been many saints in the Catholic church calendar and hundreds who have not been put in the calendar who have received the stigmata. This is simply the result of the mind and the imagination making a certain picture which is impressed upon the Etheric Double and acts, through that, on the Gross Body, this picture causing a certain disturbance, but if the disturbance is caused without any picture at all, it will likewise impress itself upon the Gross Body, and this is the way in which wounds inflicted upon the animal form of the Witch are found to manifest themselves in the human form likewise, for it must always be understood that the returning to the human form means simply the dissolving of the animal form, returning to the Magnetic Body condition and the returning into the Gross Body which has previously been left. These forms are precisely the same as the phenomena of spirit materialization, with this difference: the materialization, which is simply the Etheric Double of the medium, has been projected beyond the body and in most instances does not contain the Astral Body or any of the higher principles; it is simply the Etheric Double in a state of projection; but in Witchcraft all the other principles are within the Double, clothed with it, and in this case it is made to assume the body of some animal, when it materializes, and in the formula given in the Witchcraft books, we see how this is done, for the Witch repeats a definite formula, in which she indicates the animal form that she is going to take; thus she is able to do it through the formation of the mental picture, thus causing the Etheric substance to assume that form rather than the human, and having assumed that form, she descends to the vibratory state of gross matter. It will, therefore, be seen that such work of Witchcraft as this requires the highest magical power and the most perfect knowledge of those things, of the laws governing alchemy, magic, etc. Where the work is accomplished positively, that is to say where the guiding intelligence is that of the Witch, unless she is acting under the guidance and with the assistance of a master of the highest order, she must be one herself. Now, the majority of Witches are simply the passive tools in the hands of masters; quite often there have been other Witches or Warlocks who have helped them to do this and have ruled them, and we find in the stories of Witchcraft brought out in England, Scotland and Sweden evidences of many degrees in the Witchcraft hierarchy. They are not all equal by any means, and those who have attained great development, who are on a high plane in these dark arts, are merely the ones who have attained great powers and may assist a number of others in the performance of their works.

Again, it should be borne in mind that Dæmons quite often guide the Witches, giving them other powers, in consideration of their serving them, doing their bidding and worshipping them, in a certain sense. The stories, therefore, of compacts with the devil are true if we realize that the devil here is not Satan, but one of the minor Dæmons. Satan himself does not deal direct with the Witches, but each group of Witches may be under the control of some one of the Dæmons, and the stories point out quite clearly those particular Dæmons who may have some crotchet, the same as men, and thus make use of the Witches, assisting them in the carrying out of their designs. Sometimes, however, a Dæmon may be interested in accomplishing some great design. In this case he will deal with the Witches when he would not ordinarily do so.

The Salem Witchcraft was undoubtedly a special operation, carried on by some of the greatest Dæmons for the purpose of breaking the power of the Puritans. The afflicted girls were afflicted in order to provide the ground for the prosecution of those particular Witches; in other words, the spiritual master sacrificed the lives of some twenty of his subjects in order to turn the current of public sentiment against the Witchcraft proceedings, to make Witchcraft trials odious in the mind of the public, so that thereafter there would be no law against this crime, and that therefore the intercourse with Dæmons might go on with perfect safety in after years, and this was successful.

The various tricks that are performed, such as depositing balls of hair, sticking of pins and everything of that kind by those formula are resorted to simply as a means of fixing the picture in the mind of the Witch, so that the work of afflicting the Etheric Bodies may be carried on with greater convenience.

The reason why certain kinds of wood such as Witch Hazel and others have been associated with the practice of Witchcraft is because they have a close affinity for the Etheric Principle, and become channels through which the Magnetic Body may act upon surrounding nature with great efficiency.

The familiar of the Witch, when not an Imp, is a Dæmon who has assumed a certain form and, generally speaking, it is simply the Imp, that is, an artificial Elemental, though it may be a Dæmon of a low order who has assumed some form and is always associated with the Witch.

This intercourse with Dæmons and artificial Elementals, this life in the Etheric Double rather than in the Gross Body, develops certain principles of the being in a very undesirable way and develops in the Witch the type that has grown up and become known to literature; likewise the atmosphere of hatred in which the Witch must always live, the fact that she makes use of these powers for the purpose of reeking her vengeance, of injuring others, has the tendency to perpetually develop the worst side of her nature, until her whole character is distorted and she becomes the typical Witch. Also it should be borne in mind that the Imps compel the Witch to send them forth. As they live by the acts which they perform, they must force her to put them to work and give them something to do, these Elementals being unable to do anything on their own motion. For this reason, she is continually forced to do evil acts and is hastened on from one stage of evil doing to another.

Further, there can be no doubt that at these Witch meetings carnal intercourse takes place between the

Witches and the Dæmons who have them under their control; also when masters of a human character are the real familiars or rather the controls back of the familiars, they likewise have carnal intercourse with the Witches and by this interchange of the sex principles the relation is maintained. Adultery is, therefore, the foundation underlying the maintenance of the union between the Dæmons and the Witches. It was for this reason that witchcraft was so severely punished and justly, because it represents the union between Dæmons and human being and requires the perpetuation of this carnal intercourse in order to the successful accomplishment of the object.

The Witches are also ever ready to make others Witches, to teach the devilish art to as many as will practice it, and many of the spirit mediums who are following materialization are really becoming channels for the activity of these Dæmons of Witchcraft, to be used for the purpose of bewitching people. When you realize that many Dæmons have become devils, have absolutely no character except one of hatred to the human race, one of evil, are totally depraved, delighting in evil for its own sake, you can understand why it is that they will make use of people to gratify their propensity for evil when it does them no good. They, being the embodiment of the principle of evil, take delight in doing evil for its own sake, without deriving any other benefit from it. This is the explanation of the silly, childish element of Witchcraft, but with all this it is a terrible thing, working a terrible evil on whoever falls a victim to it.

LESSON X

CEREMONIAL MAGIC

Ceremonial Magic deals primarily with the invocation of the Devas; that is the purpose for which it is employed. The Devas are an order of spirits, something of the same order as men. They are something like the Genii of the Arabs, and their nature is brought out at considerable length in the Epics of India.

The word "Deva" literally means a shining one, a bright one. They are not on the same level as the gods, but occupy a position immeasurably above that of the Elementals. The malignant Devas or Ashuras are something like the devils of the Greeks, being of a lower order than the Dæmons, while the benevolent Devas are the same as the Shuras and are something like the Dæmons, but are all lower than the Gods.

In our usage of Dæmons here, it must be borne in mind that we use it in the Greek sense, not in the Christian or theological sense of the term.

The difference between demons and devils is mainly a difference in their character. A devil is one who is absolutely malignant, who is corrupt *per se,* delighting in evil, a natural born trouble maker, who does evil for its own sake. A Dæmon, on the other hand, is a being, ordinarily speaking, moral, or at any rate benevolent, but who will do evil in order to accomplish a purpose he may have in mind. He will consequently do evil if evil will help in carrying out his purpose. The Devil does meanness out of pure cursedness, while the Dæmon does it as a means to an end. The Dæmons may, however, be quite friendly, in a way. But it should further be observed that among many of the Greeks there was a belief in Dæmons who did not do evil. We read of good Daemons and bad Daemons, and the Stoic philosophers speak of man's spirit as the Dæmon that is within him.

A Daemon should, therefore, be understood in the sense of a spiritual being. Whether it be in a human spirit, a discarnate spirit or one who was never incarnated, it is a spiritual being; it is not a God.

The Devas represent a class of spiritual intelligences who are not under Divine guidance. They are not the angels who serve God, who do His will, niether are they the Dæmons in the Christian sense of the term, the false gods who are in opposition to the Lord's government. It is rather difficult to classify them in the light of Christian truth. They are mainly on the Mental and Astral Planes; likewise, many of them are in the Ether. They are the higher fairies of folk lore, the Fays of the Scandinavian mythology, and seem to be an order of beings who are not loyal subjects of God or of the devil either —beings of a high degree of intelligence, who are attached, in a way, to mankind, and are willing to aid man, though requiring a degree of service at his hands; their relation is mainly of a personal character. If you think of an Elemental immeasurably developed, until he is about on the plane of humanity, you will form some idea of the nature of the Devas. There is a certain degree of government among them, much more than there is among the Elementals. They are an organization, and the Devas, generally speaking, associate themselves with certain localities, become patrons of certain cities or countries; thus they become the Genius of that locality.

The Nymphs of the woods, etc., spoken of by the ancient poets, are really Devas who have associated themselves with those principles, have made them their keynote, and thus become the Genius of that locality and that element. Again, very often a Deva becomes a patron of some family, associating itself with this family, and in that case will protect any member of the family because of this personal relation he or she has to this family. The Devas are consequently not to be commanded by the Magus in the way that the Elementals are commanded, being practically on the same level as man. Sometimes they are on a much higher plane, much more powerful than the Magus, but one of them is usually equal to the Magus. Now, if in the invocation a number of them are brought to the place, it will logically follow that they will be far superior to him; that he will be completely outnumbered, completely overbalanced by the power of these Devas. Because they are really as powerful as is the Magus, it is impossible for him by a word of command to compel their presence. He must resort to some other method. This method is Ceremonial Magic. By going through certain elaborate ceremonies, forces are set in motion which will compel the presence of the Devas. All ceremonies of a magical character presented in lodges are really for the purpose of summoning the Devas. The Masonic Lodge is really a Deva temple, where they are drawn by the ceremonies. The elaborate ritual prepares everything and, if carried out in the proper form, with sufficient concentration, sufficient feeling, together with a sufficient intellectual power concentrated upon the ritual, especially if the Worshipful Master is one in possession of considerable occult knowledge and development, the Devas will be summoned, will appear in the Lodge Room and will assist in carrying out the ceremonies. There are other lodges of a Masonic character which have ceremonies for the same purpose. One such lodge is the Order of the Magi. Its ceremonies are almost exclusively for the purpose of invoking Devas. As many as fifty have been in the lodge room at one time. This is simply an illustration of all that type of lodges. The reason they are able to accomplish more than the other lodges of the same type is simply because there are real adepts in their order, that are really there. The ceremonies, if performed by adepts would bring to any lodge room these entities. These ceremonies are the means of calling these beings.

The Odd Fellows is another Order which is carrying on the same work and, whether lodge members know it or not, even though they may have lost sight of the real purpose of the ceremonies, nevertheless if sufficient force is thrown into the invocation, they will be brought there.

Let all those who do not wish to deal with Devas, eschew all lodges having ceremonies used for the purpose of generating forces. There is no ritual that is gone through merely for fun. The persons who originally formulated these rituals of the older orders were working for a definite result; that result was the invocation of super-mundane entities or Devas. The Odes employed in the various temple services are for the purpose of establishing a certain rhythm which will compel the presence of the Devas. The colors employed in lodge regalia are very often designed for this very purpose; all those combinations and symbolic figures have the same influence. In the purely Magical lodge we have a few figures that are employed quite prominently; these are usually the cross, triangle, crescent, circle, pentagram, hexagram, square, diamond, sphere and the cube; also in some, the swastika, and in the Masonic lodges, of course, the compass and square. These figures all have certain symbolic meanings. They are the product of certain rates of vibration, the effects of certain qualities in the higher realms. By looking upon them, contemplating them, their picture is formed in the imagination of all the members. As this picture is formed in the imagination, the Aura sets up the corresponding vibration. Thus, in a few moments, the atmosphere of the lodge room is charged with the vibration corresponding to the symbol. This means that the forces having the same rate of vibration are charging the room. It becomes magnetized by that particular influence appertaining to the symbols. Those forces of a particular kind are there. A magnet is thus established for all the forces of nature of this particular type, drawing them there, centering them upon the room, so that it becomes a nucleus for those forces. In this way the Devas having that keynote are drawn to the room by reason of this powerful attraction, this magnetic point. They are brought there. Thus sometimes hundreds of Devas are drawn to the room in spite of themselves. They have to appear there because of those ceremonies, while more than likely not one of them could have been brought there merely by the concentration of will of the one performing the rite, had he dispensed with all ritual.

Another important aid in Ceremonial Magic is the garments that are worn, the robes, etc., acting in the same way the symbolic figures do, symbolic colors and also the material helping to establish the rhythm that will draw the Devas.

Likewise, where incense is burned it has a great influence, for it should be borne in mind that every perfume has its occult quality, and as the odor rises from the burning incense it will set free an occult force that will draw the Devas of that particular type there.

Again, colored lights have an influence in building up the attractive force for the work.

Further, the music that may be employed has its influence; in fact, one of the greatest magical powers is in music. It draws those Devas belonging to that type, and helps to make up the rhythm. The motions that are gone through in the ceremonies impart the vibration to the ether and help more and more to establish that rhythm, all those forces working unto the accomplishment of that rhythmic attraction, the building up of the magnet which will draw the Devas there.

Now, when you draw them there, when they come in the lodge room, the real work has begun. If there is not a master present it is quite simple. The Devas are drawn there, and, of course, resent being brought there by human beings. They do not like the idea of being compelled to come by man. If the persons are negative, they take control of them. Thus the ordinary lodge practicing Ceremonial Magic comes completely under the control of the Devas who are drawn there. They take control of the minds and hearts of the persons present, in pretty much the same way as the spirit controls the medium. Such persons do not realize that they are under control; have no conception of the relation; nevertheless, they are dominated by the Devas while in the lodge.

Those lodges of a spiritistic character usually obey the Devas, yield easily and if they are sufficiently developed to recognize them, consider that they are members from the other side, and thus they are looked on as high intelligences, adepts of the order, belonging to the other side, who are thus coöperating with them, perhaps guiding them. There are lodges in existence at the present time completely dominated by those Devas, thinking them to be highly developed human beings who are at the head of the lodge. Practically every lodge purporting to be governed by spirits is thus controlled by Devas who have been invoked.

If there be one or more masters in the lodge, however, who recognize the Devas and undertake to control them, then the real struggle begins, for the Devas resent the idea of being controlled by man and will put forth all their power. It is for this reason that so many times persons in lodges have been killed; they have undertaken to control the Devas, who have resented this control and, in the struggle, the masters were not strong enough to overcome them and, therefore, have been killed.

If one is practicing Ceremonial Magic, he should at all times maintain control, should have certain ceremonies which will not only draw the Devas there but will keep them under his control. For this purpose one should draw a line, a circle, on the floor and stand within that circle. If he draw it with sufficient concentration upon the idea that it cannot be passed, he will help to build up an Auric barrier so strong that it cannot be penetrated by the Devas. By building this magic wall around him he will be protected. Then he should stand with a drawn sword in one hand, for the Devas are very much frightened at cold steel. The vehicles which they assume in coming, being of an Etheric character, are easily wounded by steel, and will thus cause them to suffer. For this reason they are afraid of the steel. The sword should be held in the hand, and in time of very great danger kept swinging around the head in circles, so that they cannot approach the person without being struck by the sword. At the same time, incense of a powerful character should be kept burning all the time. One should also wear two robes of different colors. Blue and yellow are a very fair combination, one giving power in the Mental and the other in the Astral world. This, by the way, is the source of the two robes worn by clergymen. Music should be kept up, the chanting of anthems all the time, so as to maintain the power at the highest possible point, keeping the Devas continually under control, and this should not be stopped until they have left the place. As long as the impression remains of their presence, the ceremonies should not cease.

However, it may be stated that Ceremonial Magic is never advisable. You are invoking entities more powerful than yourself, bringing them there contrary to their will, thus arousing their indignation, which is, at all times, a most dangerous practice.

Our advice is, therefore, never practice Ceremonial Magic. The only way to properly do those things is by developing yourself until you can control the entities, until you can compel them to obey you, but if you have to resort to other influences to gain sufficient power to call them, you place yourself at their mercy.

To those, however, wishing to practice Ceremonial Magic the foregoing suggestions will be of value. They really contain the key to the fundamental principles underlying the art.

A lodge room should be selected which is used for no other purpose. The regalia should never be used except for those magical ceremonies. One to perform it properly should lead a celibate life, though this is not absolutely necessary. It is much safer, however, for one who is a celibate than for one who is not. Also, it is better to live on a vegetable diet, eat sparingly, abstain from the use of intoxicating drinks if he can possibly do so, though it is often absolutely necessary for a Magus to resort to intoxicants to gain relief from the terrible strain brought on him by intercourse with the Devas. He should lead as pure and high a life as possible, and be actuated by unselfish motives, because in this way he will have much greater power to resist the encroachments of the Devas.

The room should have its altar in the east, while the Magus should stand east of the altar and there perform the ceremonies. It is better that he should know them by memory so that he will not have to read anything, but can chant them with the greatest concentration. To make the symbolic figures in the air will also be found to greatly facilitate the work.

For those wishing the formula it may be stated that the sixth and seventh Books of Moses contain some very valuable formulae; likewise, DeLaurence's Hindu Magic and Indian Occultism. The works of Paracelsus are also quite elaborate; but preëminently the manual for getting the ritual is Eliphas Levi's Dogma et Ritual de la Haut Mage, there being no other work equal to it. As Levi was excommunicated from the Order to which he belonged, by his master, for publishing the book, it is evident that it may be relied upon. No one is ever excommunicated from an Occult Brotherhood for publishing something that is not true; it is always for publishing the truth, and as Levi was excommunicated for publishing the book, it may be depended upon. Therefore, for those wishing to develop in Ceremonial Magic, we recommend the use of this book, that is, the Ritual, but at the same time would recommend them to have nothing to do with it. But then, humanity is like children; it has got to play with fire, and is looking for fire, and people can never realize the danger of Ceremonial Magic until they get hurt by fooling with it; therefore, the best thing is to tell them how to do it and let them go ahead until they learn by experience that it will not do.

LESSON XI

THEURGY

Theurgy consists in the invocation of the gods, not the invocation of the true God, but of the gods of paganism. There have been but few real theurgists in the history of the world. Probably the greatest was Iamblichus. Plotinus was also a theurgist and, to a certain extent, Porphyry, although he was opposed to the magical part —everything excepting the higher theurgy. Ammonius Saccas also practiced the art, and, to a certain degree, Apolonius of Tyana; but Greece in this period was acquainted with not more than a dozen real theurgists, and there have been but very few in any country or in any age. Paracelsus, to a certain extent, delved in theurgy, but very slightly; in fact it could not properly be said that he was a theurgist.

There are two or three reasons why it is impossible at this time to find theurgists. In the first place, it is necessary that we should learn something of the nature of the gods. They are not Dæmons in the sense in which the Greeks used the term Dæmons, neither are they Devils. They are, however, the Devils or Dæmons of Christian theology, the apostate angels who fell from their state of original purity and sanctity. Falling, they retained their angelic nature, did not descend as the true Dæmons and Devils did, becoming corrupt, but retained their purity to a certain extent, although maintaining their opposition to God and acquiring certain corrupt characteristics by reason of their rebelling against God's government.

These Dæmons aspire to worship by man. Aspiring to this worship, they undertake to procure worshippers. They became the gods of the pagan world, and in order to secure worshippers they must, of course, make it worth the while of the one who shall worship them. Thus they confer benefits upon their worshippers, becoming the patrons of certain cities and countries and doing good to those people who acknowledge them as their gods.

One to invoke these gods must, therefore, be a worshipper of them. He must believe that they are gods. This does not mean that he is to recognize them as the Supreme God, or anything of the kind, but he must at least recognize them as divine beings and must worship them individually. The mere worship of the gods in a general sense is not sufficient, but one must worship Apollo, Mars, Venus, Diana, Minerva, Cupid, if he would have their assistance, for Theurgy is used in the form of Ceremonial Magic which is resorted to for the purpose of invoking a special divine being.

A form of Theurgy is sacrifice, and the gods have certain things which they enjoy, which they like, and when those are offered on the altar they will be attracted by reason of the sacrifice. For instance, Ares can be attracted only by the offering of blood, by the offering of victims in considerable numbers. Likewise, in order to draw Persephone or her mother, Demeter, it is necessary that we offer fruit and flowers, grain, everything of that kind. If we would invoke Artemis, it is necessary that the blood of male human victims should be offered in the sacrifice either by slaying them or, as the Athenians substituted, the scourging of boys. The practice of some of the priests in scourging themselves is, therefore, for the same purpose.

Dionysus requires the blood of women, likewise wine, the vintage. In sacrificing to Apollo it is necessary that we should use nothing that has been touched by fire, but only those fruits and grains that ripen in the sun, bread baked in the sun, because those things are acceptable to him.

Likewise, the Theurgist must decide on the nature of the god he is going to invoke and must adopt that course of life which will conform to that god's character. For instance, if he choose Apollo as his patron, he must not think of eating any cooked food; he must have his food cooked by the sunshine, and must eat only those things which ripen in the sun; and if he is to invoke Demeter or Persephone he will find it advantageous to live on cereals mainly, in fact, on the fruits of the earth. If he wants to invoke Dionysus, he should live on grapes, drink wine, etc. If he invokes Ares he should eat meat principally, so as to make himself attractive, make himself the embodiment of the principle represented by the god he proposes to invoke.

Again, one to practice Theurgy must keep himself separate from the world; must have nothing to do with ordinary people, live a life of isolation and devote himself to the service of the gods primarily, believing in them, worshipping the particular one he wishes to have for his patron, adapting his whole life to the character presented in that patron. The gods require worship and love and the more fervent one's love and devotion may be the greater will be his power for drawing them. They are attracted by the zeal one has for them, and his austere fervor will bring them to him quite readily. However, it must be borne in mind that they have certain characters and certain virtues, the same as people have, and one must conform to those virtues in order to be acceptable to them. For instance, Ares will not accept the worship of a coward. One must be physically courageous if he draw Ares to him; likewise, Artemis and Athene are both virgin goddesses, consequently one must be a celibate of the purest sexual virtue if he would draw them to him. On the other hand, Aphrodite is the reverse, consequently one must be given to love, sexually speaking, himself, be rather indifferent to virtue, if he would attract Aphrodite.

Hermes, being a thief, can be drawn only by persons who are dishonest. So all the way through. If you will take the Greek and Roman Mythology and that of other nations, likewise, and study the god you wish to worship, you wish to have as your patron, find out his character and thus emulate it, try to become the very embodiment of the character of your patron, you will find that after a while you will bring yourself into that state where you will naturally create an affinity between yourself and your patron. Then, by your love, your fervor, your intense devotion, you will in time draw them to you so that they will help you; but remember, the Theurgist can never command the god or goddess, those being angels, and angels of a tolerably high order, for the lower angels sank into the realm of Dæmons and Devils. They are infinitely above man, having more powers of every description. Man, therefore, can never compel them through any of his principles. He must always remain subjective, must be negative, not positive. By becoming negative, subjective, and having the proper attitude of devotion to the patron god or goddess, it will be possible in time to draw them to you, not to compel them to come to you, but to win their approbation sufficiently to induce them to accept you as a devotee, and in time they will appear to you. At first you will receive revelations of their will, and in order to be able ultimately to work with them you must obey them. You must not have any conscientious scruples about obeying the voice of the god or goddess because it is for them to command and you to obey. The patron will never tolerate any conscience in his worshipper, but insists that his will shall be the final authority.

The patron not only has his characteristic virtues, but also his characteristic vices, and insists that they shall be performed. It is best, therefore, to select those deities who have the most perfect character, such as Athene, Hermes or Apollo. By selecting them you will have patrons who will not require you to commit very many vices, but who will insist on the virtues mainly.

It should be borne in mind further, that no one will be attractive to Athene unless he is wise, unless he has a strong sense of justice, she being the principle of Wisdom and Justice. Likewise Apollo can be attracted only by one who is artistic in a high degree. Also Hermes will be attracted only by the one who is intellectual. It is not so much the ceremonies as the character of the Theurgist that counts, for no amount of ceremony will draw the god unless the Theurgist possess the character. Likewise, he must have the devotion, the passionate love, the worshipful attitude, also a great deal of austere fervor. One to practice Theurgy must lead an ascetic life. He must have a strong will, great self control, and an unflinching character. There were so few Theurgists in the Neoplatonic time because there were so few who had the character and at the same time that fervent devotion to the gods. Apolonius of Tyana accomplished much because he was the moralist of men at his time, was austere, because he lived in temples mainly and was at the same time intensely devoted to the worship of the gods and was trying to preserve it from destruction, to save it; he was their champion, consequently his devotion and at the same time austerity of life and his high physical development enabled him to accomplish works. Ammonius Saccas was not able to do quite so much. Mentally he was philosophical, because it was not the gods so much that he was attached to as the system of philosophy preserved by the various philosophers, and the immoral gods he did not appreciate. He worked for philosophy which did not recognize their personalities as the all-important thing. Plotinus attained quite a degree of Theurgic development because he was intensely devoted to the gods, likewise led a very austere life. It was Plotinus' ideal to lead the angelic life while in the body. He regarded the body as a curse, as a clog, and tried to weaken it, so that the spirit would dominate everything, and in this process of ascetic discipline he attained a very high degree of power.

Porphyry's mind was mainly philosophical, though his devotion to the gods gave him quite a good deal of power.

Iamblichus made a specialty of the study of Theurgy and Magic, and because of the great amount of time he put in in the practice, and his devotion to the service of the gods rather than to philosophy, he brought himself in close touch with them.

Any of these methods will bring the gods to one, but it must be observed from what has been said that the elements necessary to Theurgy are:

First: A firm faith in the existence of the gods.
Second: Intense devotion to their service.
Third: Passionate love for them personally.
Fourth: Great zeal in their worship.
Fifth: An ascetically pure life.

Sixth: Austere fervor in one's attitude toward them; and

Lastly: A great deal of one's time put in in acts of w o r s h i p, contemplation, meditation, prayer, etc.

By this attitude of communion and at the smae time ready obedience to whatever promptings one receives from them, one will be able to enter into communication with them, but this is only for the one who firmly believes in them. By worshipping the gods and communing with them in the ordinary way, in the course of time one will establish a bond of attachment with them, will establish an affinity between himself and his patron so strong that his society will be sought, and in time the patron will appear to him direct. His Genius will at last be visible to him. These glimpses, through ecstasy, of the faces of the gods, were what the ancient Theurgists so longed for. The sacrifices were made unto that end, and if once they saw a glimpse of the gods they were highly gratified, regarding it as the greatest evidence of the regard of the Genius.

It is quite possible for one who believes in the gods and is devoted to them to at last enter into this Theurgic state where he can draw them to him and perform wonders by their assistance.

It should be borne in mind also that the gods are very anxious to reëstablish their worship upon the earth, and will coöperate to the full extent of their power with those who will do so, who will act as their priests and who will establish it in a proper manner; but this proper manner means that they shall be recognized as gods and shall be worshippéd as such, and they must be worshipped in accordance with their character. One must do the work that they want done. Now, if a man is willing to livĕ the life required by his particular Genius and devote himself to the service in the way that he or she will require, it is quite possible for him to become a worshipper and a real Theurgist, but one will be compelled to believe in the gods and goddesses before he can do this. It will follow logically that a Christian who recognizes the Bible position of one God alone, can never be a Theurgist. No one but a Polytheist can practice this. Although a Theurgist may believe in one Supreme God, higher than the others, one who is above the others, yet he must recognize these divine beings as having a certain individuality, who are to be served for themselves alone, not as the agents of God.

The doctrine which is growing in favor with quite a good many mystics, of worshipping the angels, is really Theurgic in its tendencies. The worship of angels does not recognize them simply as the servants of Jehovah, but as exalted beings who are worthy of worship for themselves alone, and whenever we get into this attitude we are opening the way for communion with the gods, we are thus becoming Theurgists, if we go far enough.

T. L. Harris was really a worshipper of the gods, and prepared the way for Theurgy, although he did not go far enough to really recognize it as such. Oliphant and his wife were also worshippers of the gods, but they recognized Christ too much for true Theurgists. The gods would not have very much to do with them on account of their attitude toward Christ. The nearest approach to that attitude is in Anna Kingsford and Maitland. She was really a worshipper of the gods in the true sense of the term, worshipping her Genius and teaching the worship of the Genii as the true worship. While she recognized the Supreme God, yet to her He was so far beyond everything else that we could not approach Him;

we could only worship the Genius, and her Genius was undoubtedly one of the gods. Her entire system of mysticism is not Christian in any sense of the word; it is not Oriental; it is really polytheistic and is, consequently, the open door to Theurgy. Had she been a wonder worker, had she possessed the positive force to do magical work, she would really have been a Theurgist. Instead of this, however. she was a seeress, and she was really the seeress of the gods. Her system is brought out in *The Perfect Way* and in *Clothed with the Sun* which is really the religion of the gods.

From what has been stated, the student will see the path necessary to travel if he would be a Theurgist. He will also probably realize that Theurgy is the most dangerous and the most infamous of all the types of Magic. Although requiring the highest character of all, the greatest piety, yet it is the worst of all forms; and why? It is the worship of the gods, who are angels who rebelled against the authority of Jehovah. It is consequently a going over to the worship of the enemies of Jehovah and a bold, barefaced defiance of the first commandment of the Decalogue: "Thou shalt have no other gods before me." It is the worship of other gods than Jehovah and is, hence, for the Christian, the total abandonment of the worship of God and the going off after the worship of false gods. Therefore, it is above everything else to be shunned by the man who has any care for his soul's salvation. It is treason against the God of Heaven, the acceptance of false gods, and must bring upon the one who practices it swift destruction, although to one who will follow this life, powers closely resembling the miracles performed by the Holy Ghost are quite possible.

LESSON XII

DIVINE MAGIC.

Divine Magic is that branch of Magic which is performed through the agency of the spirit of God. The principles involved are pretty much the same as in all the other aspects of magic, the difference being in the agent that is employed.

In the practice of Divine Magic we do not make use of Elementals or Thought Forms in the sense in which we do in Mental Magic, nor of Mumia or any of the other agents employed in the various branches of Magic. The spirit of God is the power employed, but the laws governing general magic are applicable to the practice of Divine Magic.

Just what do we mean by the term Divine Magic? Briefly, the art of performing miracles through the agency of the Spirit of God. The great mistake which has been made by students in the study of this subject has been the idea that the signs and wonders performed in the days of the Apostles and in the lifetime of our Lord, were special activities, were violations of the laws of nature which were never to take place afterwards; that they were special operations of the Divine fiat, out of the course and plan of things, and were performed because that was the day of miracles, but now are entirely unknown and can never be known in any time excepting that brief period. A greater mistake was never made, for it is a matter of history that the dead were raised by the prayers of the Church as late as the year 240, and also that the sick were healed much later than that. The history of the Church, as revealed in the lives of the saints, is full of thoroughly attested miracles, and we are face to face, not with a few isolated instances of miraculous activity at that time in the beginning of the Christian dispensation, but, on the contrary, with a long line of spiritual phenomena covering the history of the world in all ages. We find that in the foundation of the Jewish religion these miraculous phenomena are presented; likewise during the entire history of that people, the prophets, pretty nearly all of them, worked miracles; and we find in the lifetime of Jesus and the Apostles, instances of miracles working; further, the definite promise that He made that the power should continue, and the statement made by St. Paul that the Spirit worketh in all to profit with all; that It gives different gifts to different people; and we see miracle-working enumerated among the different gifts which the Holy Spirit was to confer upon the Church.

We are, therefore, not dealing with a few isolated phenomena, but with the workings of a general law, applicable in all ages and in all times, under all circumstances. The required circumstances and conditions being given, the miracle must, in the very nature of things, result.

What is the law governing the performance of miracles? It is the application of the Spirit of God, subject to the same general considerations and regulations which operate in the production of magical works otherwise.

When we realize that everything in the universe is, in the last analysis, a product of the Spirit of God, that it is an emanation from that Spirit, we will understand how wonderful must be the effect of that Spirit when magically employed. Stop and think for a moment what must be the result when the Spirit of God is directed unto the accomplishment of certain results, that Spirit being the source from which has come all the manifestations in the universe! If you are able to control the direction of the Spirit of God, you will, consequently, be able to control all the emanations from that spirit.

The attributes necessary to qualify one for the practice of Divine Magic are, first, a vivid imagination, enabling one to make the mental picture properly; second, a strong will, which will enable him to project this outward into manifestation; third, capacity for almost infinite concentration, which will enable the Magus to center all his power upon that one object; fourth, almost infinite patience which will prevent him from ever becoming discouraged, but will keep up the concentration for an almost infinite period of time, if necessary; fifth, unwavering faith and confidence in the result, without any shadow of doubt.

This will enable one to accomplish the magical result. Then, in addition to these attributes, he must be negatively polarized with God, in order that he may draw in and receive of that Spirit. He must, furthermore, live as nearly as possible in harmony with God, must feel the abiding presence of God, and center all his powers there. In this way, he will be able to receive of that Spirit, to become a suitable vehicle for its expression and thus to perform the work.

It must further be borne in mind that the Divine Magus must be one who has attained a mystical union with God. It is necessary that he should attain this before he does any magical work. Inasmuch as the Spirit of God is the working force employed in the magical activity, it will naturally follow that one cannot accomplish anything to speak of along those lines, until he has attained that union, until the Spirit of God is fully operative in his system. His Aura must be negatively polarized with the Divine Spirit, so that they become as one. When this has been accomplished, when he has attained to this union so that his Aura is charged with the Spirit of God, then he is able to transmit this force in any way he may see fit, providing always it be an action in harmony with the Will of God. If he attempt to do something which is antagonistic to the Will of God, he will break the affinity existing between himself and the Spirit of God; the result will be, he will cease to be the vehicle for that Spirit, will deplete himself of all spiritual power and thus will possess nothing but his own spirit, nothing but his own Aura; consequently, he will not be the Divine Magus any longer; he will be able to perform only the work of Natural Magic or Mental Magic.

The very essence of Divine Magic is, therefore, maintenance of this state of polarity with God, in order that we may be filled with His spirit.

Again, we must never be positive in our relation to God, but always negative, always receptive. If we try to direct the Divine Spirit, to command it, we shut ourselves against it, for it can never be commanded but must be sought.

It will, therefore, follow that the only way by which we may attain to this perfect union, essential to the performance of Divine Magic is by continually maintaining a state of negative polarity with God, carry out some feature of His will. It can not be too often insisted upon that the purpose of Divine Magic is the accomplishment of some essential feature of the plan of God; it is neither an activity contrary to that nor separate and apart from it. The Spirit of God, however, is unable alone, to accomplish those wonders. It is only as it operates through a human instrumentality that it is able to do the work; consequently God is quite as much dependent upon the agency of man as man is upon the Divine agency in accomplishing the work.

It must be borne in mind that the union with God is attained only by initiation. It is only as man has come into that relationship, through initiation, that he can enter this state of union. Simply willing to be one with God does not make you at one with Him in any sense whatever.

Divine Magic really bears the same general relation to true religion that the dark forms of Magic—Ceremonial and Theurgic Magic, do to the false or pagan systems of religion. It is in proportion to man's spirituality as well as his spiritual knowledge that he is able to perform these magical works, but at the same time, mere spirituality and union with God are not sufficient to enable one to perform those works. One may, for instance, attain the highest spiritual illumination and then not be able to perform works of Divine Magic or miracles. The performing of miracles is, in fact, one of the special gifts of the Holy Spirit. As it is one of those gifts which are conferred in connection with others and as a result of the reception of the Holy Spirit, it follows that all who have received the Holy Spirit do not have the gift of miracle working. It is, in fact, subject to the same general laws as the other forms of Magic, particularly Natural and Mental Magic. The performance of Magic is not simply through thought. Mere thinking does not produce Thought Forms, but thinking in conjunction with mental picturing. The more vividly the imagination is co-operating with the thinking, the more successful will one be in the production of Thought Forms. The result is, one in order to accomplish anything along this line, must exercise the power of Mental Picturing. Now, if one would employ the spirit of God in this way, he must exercise his imagination while he is polarized with the Spirit. If he has not learned to exercise his imagination, he will not be able to perform any works of magic. In performing miracles it is necessary to form a picture of the thing you wish to produce, perfect in all of its details. See the object just as you want to produce it. Then, polarizing yourself perfectly with the Spirit of God, realizing your absolute one-ness with that Spirit, losing all sense of separateness, you must see in the Spirit of God, this perfect idea and then gradually bring it down from one plane of nature to another, realizing the object, perfect in all of its details, on each plane, until at last, your concentration has brought it down to the physical. There, having realized the perfect physical expression of the object, by a last projection, you have it in open manifestation.

Anything can be created in this way. On the other hand, anything can be destroyed by dissolving it into the principles out of which it has been produced. Realize again, that the only difference between any two physical objects is a difference in the arrangement of their molecules, growing out of different rates of vibration. The different molecular elements, so-called, are simply differentiated states of vibration, resulting in different arrangement of the atoms in the molecule. Because this is the only difference, it becomes quite possible to transmute one object or one element into another, merely by a re-arrangement of its molecules, atoms or electrons, through a change in the rate of vibration. Now, how is this change to be accomplished? Simply by concentrating the attention upon it, seeing the vibrating electrons, atoms and molecules, seeing them vibrating as they really are, and then, by Mental Picturing, see the change in the vibration from that of the object or element to that of the object or element you wish to produce, and, by this change in the vibration in your own consciousness, dominate that in the object. Whenever you have succeeded in changing the rhythm, you will transmute the object into that which you wish to realize. Of course, it is rather difficult, ordinarily to do this. You must cause your Aura to change its vibration, and when the vibration is changed, to permeate the object so as to change the vibration in its Aura. You must, in other words, magnetize the object; but this may be rather difficult and the task may be greater than your Aura is able to accomplish; but when you have perfectly polarized your Aura with the Spirit of God so that it is entirely permeated by that Spirit, you can then cause the Spirit of God to assume the changed vibration, and in this way the force will be much greater than that naturally inherent in the object. The result will be a complete change in the vibration. It was in this way that Christ changed the water into wine, and accomplished all those other miracles which were of a purely alchemical character.

The dead may be raised in the same way. By changing the state of death into the rhythm of life you will accomplish the cure. Likewise by changing the discordant condition of the sick man into the perfect rhythm of health, you accomplish the greatest miracles of healing.

Whatever it may be, any change brought about in the Aura of the Magus will also result in that of the object, provided the Aura of the Magus acts upon that object with sufficient constraining force.

When the Aura is perfectly united with the Spirit of God, then the Divine Spirit responds to the changes in the vibration of the Aura, thus adding the force of the Divine Spirit to that of the Magus's Aura, thus enabling him to accomplish any work he may have in mind. But this must always be borne in mind: If he exercise this power to perform a work which is out of harmony with the Divine plan, this very attitude of mind, the concentration in order to the accomplishment of that end, will result in a disruption of the affinity existing between him and the Spirit of God, resulting in his being deserted by the latter and left to his own resources. Consequently, Divine Magic can be performed only in the accomplishment of an object in harmony with the Spirit of God.

That faith which is so essential to the performance of these works, is the perfect state of negative polarity. It is whatever is essential to preserve one's unity with the Divine Spirit, because without such spirit Divine Magic can never be accomplished, therefore, Jesus says truly, "According to your faith be it unto you." Further, "If ye have faith so much as a grain of mustard seed, ye shall say to this mountain be moved, and it shall be done, and nothing shall be impossible unto you." That is, if you have that faith which will enable you to preserve your union with God and to act, not as a separate entity, but as God.

No one can perform Divine Magic who thinks of himself in any degree separate from God at the time he is attempting to perform the great work. He must on these occasions maintain his consciousness of the absolute unity of all things. He must know that nothing in all the universe exists but God. If he can realize this truth, then he will be able to know God and to accomplish the work, for then the Spirit of God will operate in and through him, and the great work will be made possible.

Another point is, all work is accomplished by willing,

not by thinking. You may think about anything all you want to, but it is when the will speaks the word of command, when the will says ''Be'', at the same time forming a picture of the object, speaking forth the word, requiring it to be made perfect, requiring absolute realization—feeling must be thrown into the matter; it is largely emotional rather than intellectual—when the will has powerfully commanded the realization of certain things, when it has said, ''Be'' with all the power of concentration at the same time realizing the Divine Unity, the great work may be accomplished with comparative ease.

Those persons who have received the gift of Divine Magic without studying the Magical Art, are those who have developed a powerful will and a vivid imagination, in connection with the Spirit of God. That is, they are able to powerfully will, without exercising the individual will, without thinking of themselves as separate and apart from God. They have preserved unity with Him; at the same time, their will is powerful, unyielding, absolutely unwavering, and thus they are able to accomplish the work. At the same time, their imagination is most vivid, they have naturally developed those characteristics essential to prepare one for the Magical Work; they transmit the Spirit of God in this way.

Another, on the other hand, may learn the magical art, may learn how to direct these forces so that he may go at it systematically, but, of course, he must also have the will and the imagination, and at the same time maintain his perfect connection with the Divine Spirit, if he would accomplish the great work.

The all important feature in the performance of Divine Magic is a vital union with God. Without such union it is absolutely impossible for one to accomplish any results worth while, but in proportion as that union is maintained and as one has the qualities necessary to fit him for the Magical Art, and at the same time as he understands the essential features of that art, will his magical power be; but it is always advisable for us to realize that the art does not amount to anything like as much as the psychical development, the particular type of activity, and wherever that is found, no matter whether the art exists or not, the great work can be accomplished; but, of course, where the art is held in conjunction with the psychical requirements, where the particular type of being is developed in connection with the scientific knowledge, and also the presence of the spiritual union and the consciousness of that vital relationship, the work in such cases can be accomplished with much greater facility than otherwise.

No person who is not a Christian can succeed in the performance of Divine Magic, to any very great extent. This is a department of Magic which, in its successful operation is limited to mystics, to initiates, and it is just as applicable to-day as it was in the Apostolic age, being, as it is, dependent upon the operation of certain fixed laws, those laws which we have delineated in this lesson.

The reason we do not have any such miracles now as we had in the Apostolic times is simply because we do not have any such Christians now as we had then. It is the working of law, and whenever the same relation is found, we shall also find the same miraculous powers. It is the operation of the Spirit of God in conjunction with a certain type and a certain systematic direction. It was not an arbitrary fiat of the Eternal at that time, but the operation of a Divine Spiritual law, and wherever that law is found to operate, in the same way, we may expect to find the same results.

Inasmuch as miracles are the operation of a higher spiritual law, they are the same in all ages, subject only to the application of that law, and as is the miraculous law in its application, so will the result be.

RALEIGH BOOKS AND LESSONS

Complete list of the Hermetic works by Dr. A. S. Raleigh, published in book form and which will be sent postpaid at prices listed:

Woman and Super-Woman	$ 2.00
Shepherd of Men	2.50
Stanzas of Dzjn (Theogenesis)	5.00
Philosophia Hermetica	10.00
Scientifica Hermetica	10.00
Hermetic Art	10.00
Philosophy of Alchemy	10.00
Science of Alchemy	10.00
Speculative Art of Alchemy	10.00
Hermetic Science of Motion and Number	10.00
Hermetic Fundamentals Revealed	10.00
Hermetic Consciousness Unveiled	10.00
Magic	10.00

Manuscript Lessons, nicely typed and bound:

Occult Geometry	10.00
Phreno-Garten Course (explains the brain)	10.00
Metaphysical Healing (first set)	10.00
Metaphysical Healing (second set)	10.00
The Secret Sermon on the Mount or the Way of Rebirth	10.00

Other still deeper courses of Inner Lessons may be secured through direct correspondence. Also interpretations to Rudyard Kipling's "Brushwood Boy," and to his book "They," as well as interpretation to Henry Van Dyke's "The Other Wise Man." Also, interpretations to Balzac's "Magic Skin," "Louis Lambert," and "Seriphita." These are very valuable as they show how Kipling and Van Dyke received illumination in the Dream State and how Balzac got his illumination.

We also make a specialty of rare out of print books along the line of Occultism, Mysticism, the Kaballa, the Tarot, Magic, Alchemy, Symbolism, Mythology, Rosicrucianism, Hermeticism and kindred subjects. A circular showing titles and prices of our list of rare out of print books will be sent free of cost upon request.

HERMETIC PUBLISHING COMPANY

3006 Lake Park Ave.   Chicago, Ill., U. S. A.

CPSIA information can be obtained
at www.ICGtesting.com
Printed in the USA
BVHW011730150221
600169BV00005B/19